COMPANY DETAILS

COMPANY NAME:

ADDRESS=

EMAIL:

WEBSITE:

PHONE:	FAX:

EMERGENCY CONTACT PERSON:

PHONE:	EMAIL:

LOGBOOK DETAILS	COMMENTS
CONTINUED FROM LOG BOOK:	
LOG START DATE:	
CONTINUED TO LOG BOOK:	
LOG END DATE:	

CROWN JOURNALS

SHIP MAINTENANCE CHECKLIST

NAME OF SHIP:

MAKE: | MODEL:

NAME OF OWNER:

PHONE NO: | LICENSE NO:

EMAIL:

NAME OF CAPTAIN:

SIGNATURE & DATE:

GENERAL CHECKLIST

		YES	NO	N/A	COMMENTS
1	ARE OPERATING INSTRUCTIONS PROVIDED WITH IMO SYMBOLS?				
2	ARE FIRE DRILLS BEING HELD AS REQUIRED?				
3	ARE OFFICERS FAMILIAR WITH EMERGENCY STEERING GEAR?				
4					
5					
6					
7					
8					
9					
10					

LIFESAVING EQUIPMENT CHECKLIST

		YES	NO	N/A	COMMENTS
1	ARE SIDE BENCHES IN GOOD CONDITION?				
2	IS LIFEBOAT STERN FRAME IN GOOD CONDITION?				
3	ARE LIFEBOATS BILGES CLEAN?				
4	IS LIFEBOAT ENGINE IN GOOD CONDITION?				
5	ARE LIFEBOAT OARS IN GOOD CONDITION?				
6	ARE LIFEBOATS CORRECTLY STOWED IN DAVIT?				
7	HAVE DAVIT LIMIT SWITCHES BEEN TESTED?				
8					
9					
10					

FIRE FIGHTING CHECKLIST

		YES	NO	N/A	COMMENTS
1	IS THE MAIN FIRE LINE IN GOOD CONDITION?				
2	ARE A REQUIRED NUMBER OF PORTABLE FIRE EXTINGUISHERS AVAILABLE?				
3	ARE FIRE DAMPERS AND DOORS IN GOOD CONDITION?				
4	ARE FIRE ALARM AND DETECTION SYSTEMS WORKING WELL?				
5	ARE BREATHING APPARATUS IN GOOD CONDITION?				
6					
7					
8					
9					
10					

LOAD LINE CHECKLIST

		YES	NO	N/A	COMMENTS
1	ARE VENTILATORS TOGETHER WITH CLOSING APPLIANCES IN GOOD CONDITION?				
2	IS HULL FREE OF DAMAGES?				
3	ARE DRAUGHT MARKS VISIBLE?				
4	ARE AIR PIPES IN GOOD CONDITION?				
5	ARE COAMINGS AND HATCH COVERS CHECKED?				
6					
7					
8					
9					
10					

NOTES

SHIP MAINTENANCE CHECKLIST

NAME OF SHIP:	
MAKE:	MODEL:
NAME OF OWNER:	
PHONE NO:	LICENSE NO:
EMAIL:	
NAME OF CAPTAIN:	
SIGNATURE & DATE:	

GENERAL CHECKLIST

		YES	NO	N/A	COMMENTS
1	ARE OPERATING INSTRUCTIONS PROVIDED WITH IMO SYMBOLS?				
2	ARE FIRE DRILLS BEING HELD AS REQUIRED?				
3	ARE OFFICERS FAMILIAR WITH EMERGENCY STEERING GEAR?				
4					
5					
6					
7					
8					
9					
10					

LIFESAVING EQUIPMENT CHECKLIST

		YES	NO	N/A	COMMENTS
1	ARE SIDE BENCHES IN GOOD CONDITION?				
2	IS LIFEBOAT STERN FRAME IN GOOD CONDITION?				
3	ARE LIFEBOATS BILGES CLEAN?				
4	IS LIFEBOAT ENGINE IN GOOD CONDITION?				
5	ARE LIFEBOAT OARS IN GOOD CONDITION?				
6	ARE LIFEBOATS CORRECTLY STOWED IN DAVIT?				
7	HAVE DAVIT LIMIT SWITCHES BEEN TESTED?				
8					
9					
10					

FIRE FIGHTING CHECKLIST

		YES	NO	N/A	COMMENTS
1	IS THE MAIN FIRE LINE IN GOOD CONDITION?				
2	ARE A REQUIRED NUMBER OF PORTABLE FIRE EXTINGUISHERS AVAILABLE?				
3	ARE FIRE DAMPERS AND DOORS IN GOOD CONDITION?				
4	ARE FIRE ALARM AND DETECTION SYSTEMS WORKING WELL?				
5	ARE BREATHING APPARATUS IN GOOD CONDITION?				
6					
7					
8					
9					
10					

LOAD LINE CHECKLIST

		YES	NO	N/A	COMMENTS
1	ARE VENTILATORS TOGETHER WITH CLOSING APPLIANCES IN GOOD CONDITION?				
2	IS HULL FREE OF DAMAGES?				
3	ARE DRAUGHT MARKS VISIBLE?				
4	ARE AIR PIPES IN GOOD CONDITION?				
5	ARE COAMINGS AND HATCH COVERS CHECKED?				
6					
7					
8					
9					
10					

NOTES

SHIP MAINTENANCE CHECKLIST

NAME OF SHIP:	
MAKE:	MODEL:
NAME OF OWNER:	
PHONE NO:	LICENSE NO:
EMAIL:	
NAME OF CAPTAIN:	
SIGNATURE & DATE:	

GENERAL CHECKLIST

		YES	NO	N/A	COMMENTS
1	ARE OPERATING INSTRUCTIONS PROVIDED WITH IMO SYMBOLS?				
2	ARE FIRE DRILLS BEING HELD AS REQUIRED?				
3	ARE OFFICERS FAMILIAR WITH EMERGENCY STEERING GEAR?				
4					
5					
6					
7					
8					
9					
10					

LIFESAVING EQUIPMENT CHECKLIST

		YES	NO	N/A	COMMENTS
1	ARE SIDE BENCHES IN GOOD CONDITION?				
2	IS LIFEBOAT STERN FRAME IN GOOD CONDITION?				
3	ARE LIFEBOATS BILGES CLEAN?				
4	IS LIFEBOAT ENGINE IN GOOD CONDITION?				
5	ARE LIFEBOAT OARS IN GOOD CONDITION?				
6	ARE LIFEBOATS CORRECTLY STOWED IN DAVIT?				
7	HAVE DAVIT LIMIT SWITCHES BEEN TESTED?				
8					
9					
10					

FIRE FIGHTING CHECKLIST

		YES	NO	N/A	COMMENTS
1	IS THE MAIN FIRE LINE IN GOOD CONDITION?				
2	ARE A REQUIRED NUMBER OF PORTABLE FIRE EXTINGUISHERS AVAILABLE?				
3	ARE FIRE DAMPERS AND DOORS IN GOOD CONDITION?				
4	ARE FIRE ALARM AND DETECTION SYSTEMS WORKING WELL?				
5	ARE BREATHING APPARATUS IN GOOD CONDITION?				
6					
7					
8					
9					
10					

LOAD LINE CHECKLIST

		YES	NO	N/A	COMMENTS
1	ARE VENTILATORS TOGETHER WITH CLOSING APPLIANCES IN GOOD CONDITION?				
2	IS HULL FREE OF DAMAGES?				
3	ARE DRAUGHT MARKS VISIBLE?				
4	ARE AIR PIPES IN GOOD CONDITION?				
5	ARE COAMINGS AND HATCH COVERS CHECKED?				
6					
7					
8					
9					
10					

NOTES

SHIP MAINTENANCE CHECKLIST

NAME OF SHIP:	
MAKE:	MODEL:
NAME OF OWNER:	
PHONE NO:	LICENSE NO:
EMAIL:	
NAME OF CAPTAIN:	
SIGNATURE & DATE:	

GENERAL CHECKLIST

		YES	NO	N/A	COMMENTS
1	ARE OPERATING INSTRUCTIONS PROVIDED WITH IMO SYMBOLS?				
2	ARE FIRE DRILLS BEING HELD AS REQUIRED?				
3	ARE OFFICERS FAMILIAR WITH EMERGENCY STEERING GEAR?				
4					
5					
6					
7					
8					
9					
10					

LIFESAVING EQUIPMENT CHECKLIST

		YES	NO	N/A	COMMENTS
1	ARE SIDE BENCHES IN GOOD CONDITION?				
2	IS LIFEBOAT STERN FRAME IN GOOD CONDITION?				
3	ARE LIFEBOATS BILGES CLEAN?				
4	IS LIFEBOAT ENGINE IN GOOD CONDITION?				
5	ARE LIFEBOAT OARS IN GOOD CONDITION?				
6	ARE LIFEBOATS CORRECTLY STOWED IN DAVIT?				
7	HAVE DAVIT LIMIT SWITCHES BEEN TESTED?				
8					
9					
10					

FIRE FIGHTING CHECKLIST

		YES	NO	N/A	COMMENTS
1	IS THE MAIN FIRE LINE IN GOOD CONDITION?				
2	ARE A REQUIRED NUMBER OF PORTABLE FIRE EXTINGUISHERS AVAILABLE?				
3	ARE FIRE DAMPERS AND DOORS IN GOOD CONDITION?				
4	ARE FIRE ALARM AND DETECTION SYSTEMS WORKING WELL?				
5	ARE BREATHING APPARATUS IN GOOD CONDITION?				
6					
7					
8					
9					
10					

LOAD LINE CHECKLIST

		YES	NO	N/A	COMMENTS
1	ARE VENTILATORS TOGETHER WITH CLOSING APPLIANCES IN GOOD CONDITION?				
2	IS HULL FREE OF DAMAGES?				
3	ARE DRAUGHT MARKS VISIBLE?				
4	ARE AIR PIPES IN GOOD CONDITION?				
5	ARE COAMINGS AND HATCH COVERS CHECKED?				
6					
7					
8					
9					
10					

NOTES

SHIP MAINTENANCE CHECKLIST

NAME OF SHIP:	
MAKE:	MODEL:
NAME OF OWNER:	
PHONE NO:	LICENSE NO:
EMAIL:	
NAME OF CAPTAIN:	
SIGNATURE & DATE:	

GENERAL CHECKLIST

		YES	NO	N/A	COMMENTS
1	ARE OPERATING INSTRUCTIONS PROVIDED WITH IMO SYMBOLS?				
2	ARE FIRE DRILLS BEING HELD AS REQUIRED?				
3	ARE OFFICERS FAMILIAR WITH EMERGENCY STEERING GEAR?				
4					
5					
6					
7					
8					
9					
10					

LIFESAVING EQUIPMENT CHECKLIST

		YES	NO	N/A	COMMENTS
1	ARE SIDE BENCHES IN GOOD CONDITION?				
2	IS LIFEBOAT STERN FRAME IN GOOD CONDITION?				
3	ARE LIFEBOATS BILGES CLEAN?				
4	IS LIFEBOAT ENGINE IN GOOD CONDITION?				
5	ARE LIFEBOAT OARS IN GOOD CONDITION?				
6	ARE LIFEBOATS CORRECTLY STOWED IN DAVIT?				
7	HAVE DAVIT LIMIT SWITCHES BEEN TESTED?				
8					
9					
10					

FIRE FIGHTING CHECKLIST

		YES	NO	N/A	COMMENTS
1	IS THE MAIN FIRE LINE IN GOOD CONDITION?				
2	ARE A REQUIRED NUMBER OF PORTABLE FIRE EXTINGUISHERS AVAILABLE?				
3	ARE FIRE DAMPERS AND DOORS IN GOOD CONDITION?				
4	ARE FIRE ALARM AND DETECTION SYSTEMS WORKING WELL?				
5	ARE BREATHING APPARATUS IN GOOD CONDITION?				
6					
7					
8					
9					
10					

LOAD LINE CHECKLIST

		YES	NO	N/A	COMMENTS
1	ARE VENTILATORS TOGETHER WITH CLOSING APPLIANCES IN GOOD CONDITION?				
2	IS HULL FREE OF DAMAGES?				
3	ARE DRAUGHT MARKS VISIBLE?				
4	ARE AIR PIPES IN GOOD CONDITION?				
5	ARE COAMINGS AND HATCH COVERS CHECKED?				
6					
7					
8					
9					
10					

NOTES

SHIP MAINTENANCE CHECKLIST

NAME OF SHIP:

MAKE:	MODEL:

NAME OF OWNER:

PHONE NO:	LICENSE NO:

EMAIL:

NAME OF CAPTAIN:

SIGNATURE & DATE:

GENERAL CHECKLIST

		YES	NO	N/A	COMMENTS
1	ARE OPERATING INSTRUCTIONS PROVIDED WITH IMO SYMBOLS?				
2	ARE FIRE DRILLS BEING HELD AS REQUIRED?				
3	ARE OFFICERS FAMILIAR WITH EMERGENCY STEERING GEAR?				
4					
5					
6					
7					
8					
9					
10					

LIFESAVING EQUIPMENT CHECKLIST

		YES	NO	N/A	COMMENTS
1	ARE SIDE BENCHES IN GOOD CONDITION?				
2	IS LIFEBOAT STERN FRAME IN GOOD CONDITION?				
3	ARE LIFEBOATS BILGES CLEAN?				
4	IS LIFEBOAT ENGINE IN GOOD CONDITION?				
5	ARE LIFEBOAT OARS IN GOOD CONDITION?				
6	ARE LIFEBOATS CORRECTLY STOWED IN DAVIT?				
7	HAVE DAVIT LIMIT SWITCHES BEEN TESTED?				
8					
9					
10					

FIRE FIGHTING CHECKLIST

		YES	NO	N/A	COMMENTS
1	IS THE MAIN FIRE LINE IN GOOD CONDITION?				
2	ARE A REQUIRED NUMBER OF PORTABLE FIRE EXTINGUISHERS AVAILABLE?				
3	ARE FIRE DAMPERS AND DOORS IN GOOD CONDITION?				
4	ARE FIRE ALARM AND DETECTION SYSTEMS WORKING WELL?				
5	ARE BREATHING APPARATUS IN GOOD CONDITION?				
6					
7					
8					
9					
10					

LOAD LINE CHECKLIST

		YES	NO	N/A	COMMENTS
1	ARE VENTILATORS TOGETHER WITH CLOSING APPLIANCES IN GOOD CONDITION?				
2	IS HULL FREE OF DAMAGES?				
3	ARE DRAUGHT MARKS VISIBLE?				
4	ARE AIR PIPES IN GOOD CONDITION?				
5	ARE COAMINGS AND HATCH COVERS CHECKED?				
6					
7					
8					
9					
10					

NOTES

SHIP MAINTENANCE CHECKLIST

NAME OF SHIP:	
MAKE:	MODEL:
NAME OF OWNER:	
PHONE NO:	LICENSE NO:
EMAIL:	
NAME OF CAPTAIN:	
SIGNATURE & DATE:	

GENERAL CHECKLIST

		YES	NO	N/A	COMMENTS
1	ARE OPERATING INSTRUCTIONS PROVIDED WITH IMO SYMBOLS?				
2	ARE FIRE DRILLS BEING HELD AS REQUIRED?				
3	ARE OFFICERS FAMILIAR WITH EMERGENCY STEERING GEAR?				
4					
5					
6					
7					
8					
9					
10					

LIFESAVING EQUIPMENT CHECKLIST

		YES	NO	N/A	COMMENTS
1	ARE SIDE BENCHES IN GOOD CONDITION?				
2	IS LIFEBOAT STERN FRAME IN GOOD CONDITION?				
3	ARE LIFEBOATS BILGES CLEAN?				
4	IS LIFEBOAT ENGINE IN GOOD CONDITION?				
5	ARE LIFEBOAT OARS IN GOOD CONDITION?				
6	ARE LIFEBOATS CORRECTLY STOWED IN DAVIT?				
7	HAVE DAVIT LIMIT SWITCHES BEEN TESTED?				
8					
9					
10					

FIRE FIGHTING CHECKLIST

		YES	NO	N/A	COMMENTS
1	IS THE MAIN FIRE LINE IN GOOD CONDITION?				
2	ARE A REQUIRED NUMBER OF PORTABLE FIRE EXTINGUISHERS AVAILABLE?				
3	ARE FIRE DAMPERS AND DOORS IN GOOD CONDITION?				
4	ARE FIRE ALARM AND DETECTION SYSTEMS WORKING WELL?				
5	ARE BREATHING APPARATUS IN GOOD CONDITION?				
6					
7					
8					
9					
10					

LOAD LINE CHECKLIST

		YES	NO	N/A	COMMENTS
1	ARE VENTILATORS TOGETHER WITH CLOSING APPLIANCES IN GOOD CONDITION?				
2	IS HULL FREE OF DAMAGES?				
3	ARE DRAUGHT MARKS VISIBLE?				
4	ARE AIR PIPES IN GOOD CONDITION?				
5	ARE COAMINGS AND HATCH COVERS CHECKED?				
6					
7					
8					
9					
10					

NOTES

SHIP MAINTENANCE CHECKLIST

NAME OF SHIP:	
MAKE:	MODEL:
NAME OF OWNER:	
PHONE NO:	LICENSE NO:
EMAIL:	
NAME OF CAPTAIN:	
SIGNATURE & DATE:	

GENERAL CHECKLIST

		YES	NO	N/A	COMMENTS
1	ARE OPERATING INSTRUCTIONS PROVIDED WITH IMO SYMBOLS?				
2	ARE FIRE DRILLS BEING HELD AS REQUIRED?				
3	ARE OFFICERS FAMILIAR WITH EMERGENCY STEERING GEAR?				
4					
5					
6					
7					
8					
9					
10					

LIFESAVING EQUIPMENT CHECKLIST

		YES	NO	N/A	COMMENTS
1	ARE SIDE BENCHES IN GOOD CONDITION?				
2	IS LIFEBOAT STERN FRAME IN GOOD CONDITION?				
3	ARE LIFEBOATS BILGES CLEAN?				
4	IS LIFEBOAT ENGINE IN GOOD CONDITION?				
5	ARE LIFEBOAT OARS IN GOOD CONDITION?				
6	ARE LIFEBOATS CORRECTLY STOWED IN DAVIT?				
7	HAVE DAVIT LIMIT SWITCHES BEEN TESTED?				
8					
9					
10					

FIRE FIGHTING CHECKLIST

		YES	NO	N/A	COMMENTS
1	IS THE MAIN FIRE LINE IN GOOD CONDITION?				
2	ARE A REQUIRED NUMBER OF PORTABLE FIRE EXTINGUISHERS AVAILABLE?				
3	ARE FIRE DAMPERS AND DOORS IN GOOD CONDITION?				
4	ARE FIRE ALARM AND DETECTION SYSTEMS WORKING WELL?				
5	ARE BREATHING APPARATUS IN GOOD CONDITION?				
6					
7					
8					
9					
10					

LOAD LINE CHECKLIST

		YES	NO	N/A	COMMENTS
1	ARE VENTILATORS TOGETHER WITH CLOSING APPLIANCES IN GOOD CONDITION?				
2	IS HULL FREE OF DAMAGES?				
3	ARE DRAUGHT MARKS VISIBLE?				
4	ARE AIR PIPES IN GOOD CONDITION?				
5	ARE COAMINGS AND HATCH COVERS CHECKED?				
6					
7					
8					
9					
10					

NOTES

SHIP MAINTENANCE CHECKLIST

NAME OF SHIP:	
MAKE:	MODEL:
NAME OF OWNER:	
PHONE NO:	LICENSE NO:
EMAIL:	
NAME OF CAPTAIN:	
SIGNATURE & DATE:	

GENERAL CHECKLIST

		YES	NO	N/A	COMMENTS
1	ARE OPERATING INSTRUCTIONS PROVIDED WITH IMO SYMBOLS?				
2	ARE FIRE DRILLS BEING HELD AS REQUIRED?				
3	ARE OFFICERS FAMILIAR WITH EMERGENCY STEERING GEAR?				
4					
5					
6					
7					
8					
9					
10					

LIFESAVING EQUIPMENT CHECKLIST

		YES	NO	N/A	COMMENTS
1	ARE SIDE BENCHES IN GOOD CONDITION?				
2	IS LIFEBOAT STERN FRAME IN GOOD CONDITION?				
3	ARE LIFEBOATS BILGES CLEAN?				
4	IS LIFEBOAT ENGINE IN GOOD CONDITION?				
5	ARE LIFEBOAT OARS IN GOOD CONDITION?				
6	ARE LIFEBOATS CORRECTLY STOWED IN DAVIT?				
7	HAVE DAVIT LIMIT SWITCHES BEEN TESTED?				
8					
9					
10					

FIRE FIGHTING CHECKLIST

		YES	NO	N/A	COMMENTS
1	IS THE MAIN FIRE LINE IN GOOD CONDITION?				
2	ARE A REQUIRED NUMBER OF PORTABLE FIRE EXTINGUISHERS AVAILABLE?				
3	ARE FIRE DAMPERS AND DOORS IN GOOD CONDITION?				
4	ARE FIRE ALARM AND DETECTION SYSTEMS WORKING WELL?				
5	ARE BREATHING APPARATUS IN GOOD CONDITION?				
6					
7					
8					
9					
10					

LOAD LINE CHECKLIST

		YES	NO	N/A	COMMENTS
1	ARE VENTILATORS TOGETHER WITH CLOSING APPLIANCES IN GOOD CONDITION?				
2	IS HULL FREE OF DAMAGES?				
3	ARE DRAUGHT MARKS VISIBLE?				
4	ARE AIR PIPES IN GOOD CONDITION?				
5	ARE COAMINGS AND HATCH COVERS CHECKED?				
6					
7					
8					
9					
10					

NOTES

SHIP MAINTENANCE CHECKLIST

NAME OF SHIP:	
MAKE:	MODEL:
NAME OF OWNER:	
PHONE NO:	LICENSE NO:
EMAIL:	
NAME OF CAPTAIN:	
SIGNATURE & DATE:	

GENERAL CHECKLIST

		YES	NO	N/A	COMMENTS
1	ARE OPERATING INSTRUCTIONS PROVIDED WITH IMO SYMBOLS?				
2	ARE FIRE DRILLS BEING HELD AS REQUIRED?				
3	ARE OFFICERS FAMILIAR WITH EMERGENCY STEERING GEAR?				
4					
5					
6					
7					
8					
9					
10					

LIFESAVING EQUIPMENT CHECKLIST

		YES	NO	N/A	COMMENTS
1	ARE SIDE BENCHES IN GOOD CONDITION?				
2	IS LIFEBOAT STERN FRAME IN GOOD CONDITION?				
3	ARE LIFEBOATS BILGES CLEAN?				
4	IS LIFEBOAT ENGINE IN GOOD CONDITION?				
5	ARE LIFEBOAT OARS IN GOOD CONDITION?				
6	ARE LIFEBOATS CORRECTLY STOWED IN DAVIT?				
7	HAVE DAVIT LIMIT SWITCHES BEEN TESTED?				
8					
9					
10					

FIRE FIGHTING CHECKLIST

		YES	NO	N/A	COMMENTS
1	IS THE MAIN FIRE LINE IN GOOD CONDITION?				
2	ARE A REQUIRED NUMBER OF PORTABLE FIRE EXTINGUISHERS AVAILABLE?				
3	ARE FIRE DAMPERS AND DOORS IN GOOD CONDITION?				
4	ARE FIRE ALARM AND DETECTION SYSTEMS WORKING WELL?				
5	ARE BREATHING APPARATUS IN GOOD CONDITION?				
6					
7					
8					
9					
10					

LOAD LINE CHECKLIST

		YES	NO	N/A	COMMENTS
1	ARE VENTILATORS TOGETHER WITH CLOSING APPLIANCES IN GOOD CONDITION?				
2	IS HULL FREE OF DAMAGES?				
3	ARE DRAUGHT MARKS VISIBLE?				
4	ARE AIR PIPES IN GOOD CONDITION?				
5	ARE COAMINGS AND HATCH COVERS CHECKED?				
6					
7					
8					
9					
10					

NOTES

SHIP MAINTENANCE CHECKLIST

NAME OF SHIP:	
MAKE:	MODEL:
NAME OF OWNER:	
PHONE NO:	LICENSE NO:
EMAIL:	
NAME OF CAPTAIN:	
SIGNATURE & DATE:	

GENERAL CHECKLIST

		YES	NO	N/A	COMMENTS
1	ARE OPERATING INSTRUCTIONS PROVIDED WITH IMO SYMBOLS?				
2	ARE FIRE DRILLS BEING HELD AS REQUIRED?				
3	ARE OFFICERS FAMILIAR WITH EMERGENCY STEERING GEAR?				
4					
5					
6					
7					
8					
9					
10					

LIFESAVING EQUIPMENT CHECKLIST

		YES	NO	N/A	COMMENTS
1	ARE SIDE BENCHES IN GOOD CONDITION?				
2	IS LIFEBOAT STERN FRAME IN GOOD CONDITION?				
3	ARE LIFEBOATS BILGES CLEAN?				
4	IS LIFEBOAT ENGINE IN GOOD CONDITION?				
5	ARE LIFEBOAT OARS IN GOOD CONDITION?				
6	ARE LIFEBOATS CORRECTLY STOWED IN DAVIT?				
7	HAVE DAVIT LIMIT SWITCHES BEEN TESTED?				
8					
9					
10					

FIRE FIGHTING CHECKLIST

		YES	NO	N/A	COMMENTS
1	IS THE MAIN FIRE LINE IN GOOD CONDITION?				
2	ARE A REQUIRED NUMBER OF PORTABLE FIRE EXTINGUISHERS AVAILABLE?				
3	ARE FIRE DAMPERS AND DOORS IN GOOD CONDITION?				
4	ARE FIRE ALARM AND DETECTION SYSTEMS WORKING WELL?				
5	ARE BREATHING APPARATUS IN GOOD CONDITION?				
6					
7					
8					
9					
10					

LOAD LINE CHECKLIST

		YES	NO	N/A	COMMENTS
1	ARE VENTILATORS TOGETHER WITH CLOSING APPLIANCES IN GOOD CONDITION?				
2	IS HULL FREE OF DAMAGES?				
3	ARE DRAUGHT MARKS VISIBLE?				
4	ARE AIR PIPES IN GOOD CONDITION?				
5	ARE COAMINGS AND HATCH COVERS CHECKED?				
6					
7					
8					
9					
10					

NOTES

SHIP MAINTENANCE CHECKLIST

NAME OF SHIP:	
MAKE:	MODEL:
NAME OF OWNER:	
PHONE NO:	LICENSE NO:
EMAIL:	
NAME OF CAPTAIN:	
SIGNATURE & DATE:	

GENERAL CHECKLIST

		YES	NO	N/A	COMMENTS
1	ARE OPERATING INSTRUCTIONS PROVIDED WITH IMO SYMBOLS?				
2	ARE FIRE DRILLS BEING HELD AS REQUIRED?				
3	ARE OFFICERS FAMILIAR WITH EMERGENCY STEERING GEAR?				
4					
5					
6					
7					
8					
9					
10					

LIFESAVING EQUIPMENT CHECKLIST

		YES	NO	N/A	COMMENTS
1	ARE SIDE BENCHES IN GOOD CONDITION?				
2	IS LIFEBOAT STERN FRAME IN GOOD CONDITION?				
3	ARE LIFEBOATS BILGES CLEAN?				
4	IS LIFEBOAT ENGINE IN GOOD CONDITION?				
5	ARE LIFEBOAT OARS IN GOOD CONDITION?				
6	ARE LIFEBOATS CORRECTLY STOWED IN DAVIT?				
7	HAVE DAVIT LIMIT SWITCHES BEEN TESTED?				
8					
9					
10					

FIRE FIGHTING CHECKLIST

		YES	NO	N/A	COMMENTS
1	IS THE MAIN FIRE LINE IN GOOD CONDITION?				
2	ARE A REQUIRED NUMBER OF PORTABLE FIRE EXTINGUISHERS AVAILABLE?				
3	ARE FIRE DAMPERS AND DOORS IN GOOD CONDITION?				
4	ARE FIRE ALARM AND DETECTION SYSTEMS WORKING WELL?				
5	ARE BREATHING APPARATUS IN GOOD CONDITION?				
6					
7					
8					
9					
10					

LOAD LINE CHECKLIST

		YES	NO	N/A	COMMENTS
1	ARE VENTILATORS TOGETHER WITH CLOSING APPLIANCES IN GOOD CONDITION?				
2	IS HULL FREE OF DAMAGES?				
3	ARE DRAUGHT MARKS VISIBLE?				
4	ARE AIR PIPES IN GOOD CONDITION?				
5	ARE COAMINGS AND HATCH COVERS CHECKED?				
6					
7					
8					
9					
10					

NOTES

SHIP MAINTENANCE CHECKLIST

NAME OF SHIP:	
MAKE:	MODEL:
NAME OF OWNER:	
PHONE NO:	LICENSE NO:
EMAIL:	
NAME OF CAPTAIN:	
SIGNATURE & DATE:	

GENERAL CHECKLIST

		YES	NO	N/A	COMMENTS
1	ARE OPERATING INSTRUCTIONS PROVIDED WITH IMO SYMBOLS?				
2	ARE FIRE DRILLS BEING HELD AS REQUIRED?				
3	ARE OFFICERS FAMILIAR WITH EMERGENCY STEERING GEAR?				
4					
5					
6					
7					
8					
9					
10					

LIFESAVING EQUIPMENT CHECKLIST

		YES	NO	N/A	COMMENTS
1	ARE SIDE BENCHES IN GOOD CONDITION?				
2	IS LIFEBOAT STERN FRAME IN GOOD CONDITION?				
3	ARE LIFEBOATS BILGES CLEAN?				
4	IS LIFEBOAT ENGINE IN GOOD CONDITION?				
5	ARE LIFEBOAT OARS IN GOOD CONDITION?				
6	ARE LIFEBOATS CORRECTLY STOWED IN DAVIT?				
7	HAVE DAVIT LIMIT SWITCHES BEEN TESTED?				
8					
9					
10					

FIRE FIGHTING CHECKLIST

		YES	NO	N/A	COMMENTS
1	IS THE MAIN FIRE LINE IN GOOD CONDITION?				
2	ARE A REQUIRED NUMBER OF PORTABLE FIRE EXTINGUISHERS AVAILABLE?				
3	ARE FIRE DAMPERS AND DOORS IN GOOD CONDITION?				
4	ARE FIRE ALARM AND DETECTION SYSTEMS WORKING WELL?				
5	ARE BREATHING APPARATUS IN GOOD CONDITION?				
6					
7					
8					
9					
10					

LOAD LINE CHECKLIST

		YES	NO	N/A	COMMENTS
1	ARE VENTILATORS TOGETHER WITH CLOSING APPLIANCES IN GOOD CONDITION?				
2	IS HULL FREE OF DAMAGES?				
3	ARE DRAUGHT MARKS VISIBLE?				
4	ARE AIR PIPES IN GOOD CONDITION?				
5	ARE COAMINGS AND HATCH COVERS CHECKED?				
6					
7					
8					
9					
10					

NOTES

SHIP MAINTENANCE CHECKLIST

NAME OF SHIP:	

MAKE:	MODEL:

NAME OF OWNER:

PHONE NO:	LICENSE NO:

EMAIL:

NAME OF CAPTAIN:

SIGNATURE & DATE:

GENERAL CHECKLIST

		YES	NO	N/A	COMMENTS
1	ARE OPERATING INSTRUCTIONS PROVIDED WITH IMO SYMBOLS?				
2	ARE FIRE DRILLS BEING HELD AS REQUIRED?				
3	ARE OFFICERS FAMILIAR WITH EMERGENCY STEERING GEAR?				
4					
5					
6					
7					
8					
9					
10					

LIFESAVING EQUIPMENT CHECKLIST

		YES	NO	N/A	COMMENTS
1	ARE SIDE BENCHES IN GOOD CONDITION?				
2	IS LIFEBOAT STERN FRAME IN GOOD CONDITION?				
3	ARE LIFEBOATS BILGES CLEAN?				
4	IS LIFEBOAT ENGINE IN GOOD CONDITION?				
5	ARE LIFEBOAT OARS IN GOOD CONDITION?				
6	ARE LIFEBOATS CORRECTLY STOWED IN DAVIT?				
7	HAVE DAVIT LIMIT SWITCHES BEEN TESTED?				
8					
9					
10					

FIRE FIGHTING CHECKLIST

		YES	NO	N/A	COMMENTS
1	IS THE MAIN FIRE LINE IN GOOD CONDITION?				
2	ARE A REQUIRED NUMBER OF PORTABLE FIRE EXTINGUISHERS AVAILABLE?				
3	ARE FIRE DAMPERS AND DOORS IN GOOD CONDITION?				
4	ARE FIRE ALARM AND DETECTION SYSTEMS WORKING WELL?				
5	ARE BREATHING APPARATUS IN GOOD CONDITION?				
6					
7					
8					
9					
10					

LOAD LINE CHECKLIST

		YES	NO	N/A	COMMENTS
1	ARE VENTILATORS TOGETHER WITH CLOSING APPLIANCES IN GOOD CONDITION?				
2	IS HULL FREE OF DAMAGES?				
3	ARE DRAUGHT MARKS VISIBLE?				
4	ARE AIR PIPES IN GOOD CONDITION?				
5	ARE COAMINGS AND HATCH COVERS CHECKED?				
6					
7					
8					
9					
10					

NOTES

SHIP MAINTENANCE CHECKLIST

NAME OF SHIP:	
MAKE:	MODEL:
NAME OF OWNER:	
PHONE NO:	LICENSE NO:
EMAIL:	
NAME OF CAPTAIN:	
SIGNATURE & DATE:	

GENERAL CHECKLIST

		YES	NO	N/A	COMMENTS
1	ARE OPERATING INSTRUCTIONS PROVIDED WITH IMO SYMBOLS?				
2	ARE FIRE DRILLS BEING HELD AS REQUIRED?				
3	ARE OFFICERS FAMILIAR WITH EMERGENCY STEERING GEAR?				
4					
5					
6					
7					
8					
9					
10					

LIFESAVING EQUIPMENT CHECKLIST

		YES	NO	N/A	COMMENTS
1	ARE SIDE BENCHES IN GOOD CONDITION?				
2	IS LIFEBOAT STERN FRAME IN GOOD CONDITION?				
3	ARE LIFEBOATS BILGES CLEAN?				
4	IS LIFEBOAT ENGINE IN GOOD CONDITION?				
5	ARE LIFEBOAT OARS IN GOOD CONDITION?				
6	ARE LIFEBOATS CORRECTLY STOWED IN DAVIT?				
7	HAVE DAVIT LIMIT SWITCHES BEEN TESTED?				
8					
9					
10					

FIRE FIGHTING CHECKLIST

		YES	NO	N/A	COMMENTS
1	IS THE MAIN FIRE LINE IN GOOD CONDITION?				
2	ARE A REQUIRED NUMBER OF PORTABLE FIRE EXTINGUISHERS AVAILABLE?				
3	ARE FIRE DAMPERS AND DOORS IN GOOD CONDITION?				
4	ARE FIRE ALARM AND DETECTION SYSTEMS WORKING WELL?				
5	ARE BREATHING APPARATUS IN GOOD CONDITION?				
6					
7					
8					
9					
10					

LOAD LINE CHECKLIST

		YES	NO	N/A	COMMENTS
1	ARE VENTILATORS TOGETHER WITH CLOSING APPLIANCES IN GOOD CONDITION?				
2	IS HULL FREE OF DAMAGES?				
3	ARE DRAUGHT MARKS VISIBLE?				
4	ARE AIR PIPES IN GOOD CONDITION?				
5	ARE COAMINGS AND HATCH COVERS CHECKED?				
6					
7					
8					
9					
10					

NOTES

SHIP MAINTENANCE CHECKLIST

NAME OF SHIP:	
MAKE:	MODEL:
NAME OF OWNER:	
PHONE NO:	LICENSE NO:
EMAIL:	
NAME OF CAPTAIN:	
SIGNATURE & DATE:	

GENERAL CHECKLIST

		YES	NO	N/A	COMMENTS
1	ARE OPERATING INSTRUCTIONS PROVIDED WITH IMO SYMBOLS?				
2	ARE FIRE DRILLS BEING HELD AS REQUIRED?				
3	ARE OFFICERS FAMILIAR WITH EMERGENCY STEERING GEAR?				
4					
5					
6					
7					
8					
9					
10					

LIFESAVING EQUIPMENT CHECKLIST

		YES	NO	N/A	COMMENTS
1	ARE SIDE BENCHES IN GOOD CONDITION?				
2	IS LIFEBOAT STERN FRAME IN GOOD CONDITION?				
3	ARE LIFEBOATS BILGES CLEAN?				
4	IS LIFEBOAT ENGINE IN GOOD CONDITION?				
5	ARE LIFEBOAT OARS IN GOOD CONDITION?				
6	ARE LIFEBOATS CORRECTLY STOWED IN DAVIT?				
7	HAVE DAVIT LIMIT SWITCHES BEEN TESTED?				
8					
9					
10					

FIRE FIGHTING CHECKLIST

		YES	NO	N/A	COMMENTS
1	IS THE MAIN FIRE LINE IN GOOD CONDITION?				
2	ARE A REQUIRED NUMBER OF PORTABLE FIRE EXTINGUISHERS AVAILABLE?				
3	ARE FIRE DAMPERS AND DOORS IN GOOD CONDITION?				
4	ARE FIRE ALARM AND DETECTION SYSTEMS WORKING WELL?				
5	ARE BREATHING APPARATUS IN GOOD CONDITION?				
6					
7					
8					
9					
10					

LOAD LINE CHECKLIST

		YES	NO	N/A	COMMENTS
1	ARE VENTILATORS TOGETHER WITH CLOSING APPLIANCES IN GOOD CONDITION?				
2	IS HULL FREE OF DAMAGES?				
3	ARE DRAUGHT MARKS VISIBLE?				
4	ARE AIR PIPES IN GOOD CONDITION?				
5	ARE COAMINGS AND HATCH COVERS CHECKED?				
6					
7					
8					
9					
10					

NOTES

SHIP MAINTENANCE CHECKLIST

NAME OF SHIP:	

MAKE:	MODEL:

NAME OF OWNER:

PHONE NO:	LICENSE NO:

EMAIL:

NAME OF CAPTAIN:

SIGNATURE & DATE:

GENERAL CHECKLIST

		YES	NO	N/A	COMMENTS
1	ARE OPERATING INSTRUCTIONS PROVIDED WITH IMO SYMBOLS?				
2	ARE FIRE DRILLS BEING HELD AS REQUIRED?				
3	ARE OFFICERS FAMILIAR WITH EMERGENCY STEERING GEAR?				
4					
5					
6					
7					
8					
9					
10					

LIFESAVING EQUIPMENT CHECKLIST

		YES	NO	N/A	COMMENTS
1	ARE SIDE BENCHES IN GOOD CONDITION?				
2	IS LIFEBOAT STERN FRAME IN GOOD CONDITION?				
3	ARE LIFEBOATS BILGES CLEAN?				
4	IS LIFEBOAT ENGINE IN GOOD CONDITION?				
5	ARE LIFEBOAT OARS IN GOOD CONDITION?				
6	ARE LIFEBOATS CORRECTLY STOWED IN DAVIT?				
7	HAVE DAVIT LIMIT SWITCHES BEEN TESTED?				
8					
9					
10					

FIRE FIGHTING CHECKLIST

		YES	NO	N/A	COMMENTS
1	IS THE MAIN FIRE LINE IN GOOD CONDITION?				
2	ARE A REQUIRED NUMBER OF PORTABLE FIRE EXTINGUISHERS AVAILABLE?				
3	ARE FIRE DAMPERS AND DOORS IN GOOD CONDITION?				
4	ARE FIRE ALARM AND DETECTION SYSTEMS WORKING WELL?				
5	ARE BREATHING APPARATUS IN GOOD CONDITION?				
6					
7					
8					
9					
10					

LOAD LINE CHECKLIST

		YES	NO	N/A	COMMENTS
1	ARE VENTILATORS TOGETHER WITH CLOSING APPLIANCES IN GOOD CONDITION?				
2	IS HULL FREE OF DAMAGES?				
3	ARE DRAUGHT MARKS VISIBLE?				
4	ARE AIR PIPES IN GOOD CONDITION?				
5	ARE COAMINGS AND HATCH COVERS CHECKED?				
6					
7					
8					
9					
10					

NOTES

SHIP MAINTENANCE CHECKLIST

NAME OF SHIP:	
MAKE:	MODEL:
NAME OF OWNER:	
PHONE NO:	LICENSE NO:
EMAIL:	
NAME OF CAPTAIN:	
SIGNATURE & DATE:	

GENERAL CHECKLIST

		YES	NO	N/A	COMMENTS
1	ARE OPERATING INSTRUCTIONS PROVIDED WITH IMO SYMBOLS?				
2	ARE FIRE DRILLS BEING HELD AS REQUIRED?				
3	ARE OFFICERS FAMILIAR WITH EMERGENCY STEERING GEAR?				
4					
5					
6					
7					
8					
9					
10					

LIFESAVING EQUIPMENT CHECKLIST

		YES	NO	N/A	COMMENTS
1	ARE SIDE BENCHES IN GOOD CONDITION?				
2	IS LIFEBOAT STERN FRAME IN GOOD CONDITION?				
3	ARE LIFEBOATS BILGES CLEAN?				
4	IS LIFEBOAT ENGINE IN GOOD CONDITION?				
5	ARE LIFEBOAT OARS IN GOOD CONDITION?				
6	ARE LIFEBOATS CORRECTLY STOWED IN DAVIT?				
7	HAVE DAVIT LIMIT SWITCHES BEEN TESTED?				
8					
9					
10					

FIRE FIGHTING CHECKLIST

		YES	NO	N/A	COMMENTS
1	IS THE MAIN FIRE LINE IN GOOD CONDITION?				
2	ARE A REQUIRED NUMBER OF PORTABLE FIRE EXTINGUISHERS AVAILABLE?				
3	ARE FIRE DAMPERS AND DOORS IN GOOD CONDITION?				
4	ARE FIRE ALARM AND DETECTION SYSTEMS WORKING WELL?				
5	ARE BREATHING APPARATUS IN GOOD CONDITION?				
6					
7					
8					
9					
10					

LOAD LINE CHECKLIST

		YES	NO	N/A	COMMENTS
1	ARE VENTILATORS TOGETHER WITH CLOSING APPLIANCES IN GOOD CONDITION?				
2	IS HULL FREE OF DAMAGES?				
3	ARE DRAUGHT MARKS VISIBLE?				
4	ARE AIR PIPES IN GOOD CONDITION?				
5	ARE COAMINGS AND HATCH COVERS CHECKED?				
6					
7					
8					
9					
10					

NOTES

SHIP MAINTENANCE CHECKLIST

NAME OF SHIP:	
MAKE:	MODEL:
NAME OF OWNER:	
PHONE NO:	LICENSE NO:
EMAIL:	
NAME OF CAPTAIN:	
SIGNATURE & DATE:	

GENERAL CHECKLIST

		YES	NO	N/A	COMMENTS
1	ARE OPERATING INSTRUCTIONS PROVIDED WITH IMO SYMBOLS?				
2	ARE FIRE DRILLS BEING HELD AS REQUIRED?				
3	ARE OFFICERS FAMILIAR WITH EMERGENCY STEERING GEAR?				
4					
5					
6					
7					
8					
9					
10					

LIFESAVING EQUIPMENT CHECKLIST

		YES	NO	N/A	COMMENTS
1	ARE SIDE BENCHES IN GOOD CONDITION?				
2	IS LIFEBOAT STERN FRAME IN GOOD CONDITION?				
3	ARE LIFEBOATS BILGES CLEAN?				
4	IS LIFEBOAT ENGINE IN GOOD CONDITION?				
5	ARE LIFEBOAT OARS IN GOOD CONDITION?				
6	ARE LIFEBOATS CORRECTLY STOWED IN DAVIT?				
7	HAVE DAVIT LIMIT SWITCHES BEEN TESTED?				
8					
9					
10					

FIRE FIGHTING CHECKLIST

		YES	NO	N/A	COMMENTS
1	IS THE MAIN FIRE LINE IN GOOD CONDITION?				
2	ARE A REQUIRED NUMBER OF PORTABLE FIRE EXTINGUISHERS AVAILABLE?				
3	ARE FIRE DAMPERS AND DOORS IN GOOD CONDITION?				
4	ARE FIRE ALARM AND DETECTION SYSTEMS WORKING WELL?				
5	ARE BREATHING APPARATUS IN GOOD CONDITION?				
6					
7					
8					
9					
10					

LOAD LINE CHECKLIST

		YES	NO	N/A	COMMENTS
1	ARE VENTILATORS TOGETHER WITH CLOSING APPLIANCES IN GOOD CONDITION?				
2	IS HULL FREE OF DAMAGES?				
3	ARE DRAUGHT MARKS VISIBLE?				
4	ARE AIR PIPES IN GOOD CONDITION?				
5	ARE COAMINGS AND HATCH COVERS CHECKED?				
6					
7					
8					
9					
10					

NOTES

SHIP MAINTENANCE CHECKLIST

NAME OF SHIP:	
MAKE:	MODEL:
NAME OF OWNER:	
PHONE NO:	LICENSE NO:
EMAIL:	
NAME OF CAPTAIN:	
SIGNATURE & DATE:	

GENERAL CHECKLIST

		YES	NO	N/A	COMMENTS
1	ARE OPERATING INSTRUCTIONS PROVIDED WITH IMO SYMBOLS?				
2	ARE FIRE DRILLS BEING HELD AS REQUIRED?				
3	ARE OFFICERS FAMILIAR WITH EMERGENCY STEERING GEAR?				
4					
5					
6					
7					
8					
9					
10					

LIFESAVING EQUIPMENT CHECKLIST

		YES	NO	N/A	COMMENTS
1	ARE SIDE BENCHES IN GOOD CONDITION?				
2	IS LIFEBOAT STERN FRAME IN GOOD CONDITION?				
3	ARE LIFEBOATS BILGES CLEAN?				
4	IS LIFEBOAT ENGINE IN GOOD CONDITION?				
5	ARE LIFEBOAT OARS IN GOOD CONDITION?				
6	ARE LIFEBOATS CORRECTLY STOWED IN DAVIT?				
7	HAVE DAVIT LIMIT SWITCHES BEEN TESTED?				
8					
9					
10					

FIRE FIGHTING CHECKLIST

		YES	NO	N/A	COMMENTS
1	IS THE MAIN FIRE LINE IN GOOD CONDITION?				
2	ARE A REQUIRED NUMBER OF PORTABLE FIRE EXTINGUISHERS AVAILABLE?				
3	ARE FIRE DAMPERS AND DOORS IN GOOD CONDITION?				
4	ARE FIRE ALARM AND DETECTION SYSTEMS WORKING WELL?				
5	ARE BREATHING APPARATUS IN GOOD CONDITION?				
6					
7					
8					
9					
10					

LOAD LINE CHECKLIST

		YES	NO	N/A	COMMENTS
1	ARE VENTILATORS TOGETHER WITH CLOSING APPLIANCES IN GOOD CONDITION?				
2	IS HULL FREE OF DAMAGES?				
3	ARE DRAUGHT MARKS VISIBLE?				
4	ARE AIR PIPES IN GOOD CONDITION?				
5	ARE COAMINGS AND HATCH COVERS CHECKED?				
6					
7					
8					
9					
10					

NOTES

SHIP MAINTENANCE CHECKLIST

NAME OF SHIP:	
MAKE:	MODEL:
NAME OF OWNER:	
PHONE NO:	LICENSE NO:
EMAIL:	
NAME OF CAPTAIN:	
SIGNATURE & DATE:	

GENERAL CHECKLIST

		YES	NO	N/A	COMMENTS
1	ARE OPERATING INSTRUCTIONS PROVIDED WITH IMO SYMBOLS?				
2	ARE FIRE DRILLS BEING HELD AS REQUIRED?				
3	ARE OFFICERS FAMILIAR WITH EMERGENCY STEERING GEAR?				
4					
5					
6					
7					
8					
9					
10					

LIFESAVING EQUIPMENT CHECKLIST

		YES	NO	N/A	COMMENTS
1	ARE SIDE BENCHES IN GOOD CONDITION?				
2	IS LIFEBOAT STERN FRAME IN GOOD CONDITION?				
3	ARE LIFEBOATS BILGES CLEAN?				
4	IS LIFEBOAT ENGINE IN GOOD CONDITION?				
5	ARE LIFEBOAT OARS IN GOOD CONDITION?				
6	ARE LIFEBOATS CORRECTLY STOWED IN DAVIT?				
7	HAVE DAVIT LIMIT SWITCHES BEEN TESTED?				
8					
9					
10					

FIRE FIGHTING CHECKLIST

		YES	NO	N/A	COMMENTS
1	IS THE MAIN FIRE LINE IN GOOD CONDITION?				
2	ARE A REQUIRED NUMBER OF PORTABLE FIRE EXTINGUISHERS AVAILABLE?				
3	ARE FIRE DAMPERS AND DOORS IN GOOD CONDITION?				
4	ARE FIRE ALARM AND DETECTION SYSTEMS WORKING WELL?				
5	ARE BREATHING APPARATUS IN GOOD CONDITION?				
6					
7					
8					
9					
10					

LOAD LINE CHECKLIST

		YES	NO	N/A	COMMENTS
1	ARE VENTILATORS TOGETHER WITH CLOSING APPLIANCES IN GOOD CONDITION?				
2	IS HULL FREE OF DAMAGES?				
3	ARE DRAUGHT MARKS VISIBLE?				
4	ARE AIR PIPES IN GOOD CONDITION?				
5	ARE COAMINGS AND HATCH COVERS CHECKED?				
6					
7					
8					
9					
10					

NOTES

SHIP MAINTENANCE CHECKLIST

NAME OF SHIP:	
MAKE:	MODEL:
NAME OF OWNER:	
PHONE NO:	LICENSE NO:
EMAIL:	
NAME OF CAPTAIN:	
SIGNATURE & DATE:	

GENERAL CHECKLIST

		YES	NO	N/A	COMMENTS
1	ARE OPERATING INSTRUCTIONS PROVIDED WITH IMO SYMBOLS?				
2	ARE FIRE DRILLS BEING HELD AS REQUIRED?				
3	ARE OFFICERS FAMILIAR WITH EMERGENCY STEERING GEAR?				
4					
5					
6					
7					
8					
9					
10					

LIFESAVING EQUIPMENT CHECKLIST

		YES	NO	N/A	COMMENTS
1	ARE SIDE BENCHES IN GOOD CONDITION?				
2	IS LIFEBOAT STERN FRAME IN GOOD CONDITION?				
3	ARE LIFEBOATS BILGES CLEAN?				
4	IS LIFEBOAT ENGINE IN GOOD CONDITION?				
5	ARE LIFEBOAT OARS IN GOOD CONDITION?				
6	ARE LIFEBOATS CORRECTLY STOWED IN DAVIT?				
7	HAVE DAVIT LIMIT SWITCHES BEEN TESTED?				
8					
9					
10					

FIRE FIGHTING CHECKLIST

		YES	NO	N/A	COMMENTS
1	IS THE MAIN FIRE LINE IN GOOD CONDITION?				
2	ARE A REQUIRED NUMBER OF PORTABLE FIRE EXTINGUISHERS AVAILABLE?				
3	ARE FIRE DAMPERS AND DOORS IN GOOD CONDITION?				
4	ARE FIRE ALARM AND DETECTION SYSTEMS WORKING WELL?				
5	ARE BREATHING APPARATUS IN GOOD CONDITION?				
6					
7					
8					
9					
10					

LOAD LINE CHECKLIST

		YES	NO	N/A	COMMENTS
1	ARE VENTILATORS TOGETHER WITH CLOSING APPLIANCES IN GOOD CONDITION?				
2	IS HULL FREE OF DAMAGES?				
3	ARE DRAUGHT MARKS VISIBLE?				
4	ARE AIR PIPES IN GOOD CONDITION?				
5	ARE COAMINGS AND HATCH COVERS CHECKED?				
6					
7					
8					
9					
10					

NOTES

SHIP MAINTENANCE CHECKLIST

NAME OF SHIP:

MAKE:	MODEL:

NAME OF OWNER:

PHONE NO:	LICENSE NO:

EMAIL:

NAME OF CAPTAIN:

SIGNATURE & DATE:

GENERAL CHECKLIST

		YES	NO	N/A	COMMENTS
1	ARE OPERATING INSTRUCTIONS PROVIDED WITH IMO SYMBOLS?				
2	ARE FIRE DRILLS BEING HELD AS REQUIRED?				
3	ARE OFFICERS FAMILIAR WITH EMERGENCY STEERING GEAR?				
4					
5					
6					
7					
8					
9					
10					

LIFESAVING EQUIPMENT CHECKLIST

		YES	NO	N/A	COMMENTS
1	ARE SIDE BENCHES IN GOOD CONDITION?				
2	IS LIFEBOAT STERN FRAME IN GOOD CONDITION?				
3	ARE LIFEBOATS BILGES CLEAN?				
4	IS LIFEBOAT ENGINE IN GOOD CONDITION?				
5	ARE LIFEBOAT OARS IN GOOD CONDITION?				
6	ARE LIFEBOATS CORRECTLY STOWED IN DAVIT?				
7	HAVE DAVIT LIMIT SWITCHES BEEN TESTED?				
8					
9					
10					

FIRE FIGHTING CHECKLIST

		YES	NO	N/A	COMMENTS
1	IS THE MAIN FIRE LINE IN GOOD CONDITION?				
2	ARE A REQUIRED NUMBER OF PORTABLE FIRE EXTINGUISHERS AVAILABLE?				
3	ARE FIRE DAMPERS AND DOORS IN GOOD CONDITION?				
4	ARE FIRE ALARM AND DETECTION SYSTEMS WORKING WELL?				
5	ARE BREATHING APPARATUS IN GOOD CONDITION?				
6					
7					
8					
9					
10					

LOAD LINE CHECKLIST

		YES	NO	N/A	COMMENTS
1	ARE VENTILATORS TOGETHER WITH CLOSING APPLIANCES IN GOOD CONDITION?				
2	IS HULL FREE OF DAMAGES?				
3	ARE DRAUGHT MARKS VISIBLE?				
4	ARE AIR PIPES IN GOOD CONDITION?				
5	ARE COAMINGS AND HATCH COVERS CHECKED?				
6					
7					
8					
9					
10					

NOTES

SHIP MAINTENANCE CHECKLIST

NAME OF SHIP:	
MAKE:	MODEL:
NAME OF OWNER:	
PHONE NO:	LICENSE NO:
EMAIL:	
NAME OF CAPTAIN:	
SIGNATURE & DATE:	

GENERAL CHECKLIST

		YES	NO	N/A	COMMENTS
1	ARE OPERATING INSTRUCTIONS PROVIDED WITH IMO SYMBOLS?				
2	ARE FIRE DRILLS BEING HELD AS REQUIRED?				
3	ARE OFFICERS FAMILIAR WITH EMERGENCY STEERING GEAR?				
4					
5					
6					
7					
8					
9					
10					

LIFESAVING EQUIPMENT CHECKLIST

		YES	NO	N/A	COMMENTS
1	ARE SIDE BENCHES IN GOOD CONDITION?				
2	IS LIFEBOAT STERN FRAME IN GOOD CONDITION?				
3	ARE LIFEBOATS BILGES CLEAN?				
4	IS LIFEBOAT ENGINE IN GOOD CONDITION?				
5	ARE LIFEBOAT OARS IN GOOD CONDITION?				
6	ARE LIFEBOATS CORRECTLY STOWED IN DAVIT?				
7	HAVE DAVIT LIMIT SWITCHES BEEN TESTED?				
8					
9					
10					

FIRE FIGHTING CHECKLIST

		YES	NO	N/A	COMMENTS
1	IS THE MAIN FIRE LINE IN GOOD CONDITION?				
2	ARE A REQUIRED NUMBER OF PORTABLE FIRE EXTINGUISHERS AVAILABLE?				
3	ARE FIRE DAMPERS AND DOORS IN GOOD CONDITION?				
4	ARE FIRE ALARM AND DETECTION SYSTEMS WORKING WELL?				
5	ARE BREATHING APPARATUS IN GOOD CONDITION?				
6					
7					
8					
9					
10					

LOAD LINE CHECKLIST

		YES	NO	N/A	COMMENTS
1	ARE VENTILATORS TOGETHER WITH CLOSING APPLIANCES IN GOOD CONDITION?				
2	IS HULL FREE OF DAMAGES?				
3	ARE DRAUGHT MARKS VISIBLE?				
4	ARE AIR PIPES IN GOOD CONDITION?				
5	ARE COAMINGS AND HATCH COVERS CHECKED?				
6					
7					
8					
9					
10					

NOTES

SHIP MAINTENANCE CHECKLIST

NAME OF SHIP:

MAKE: | MODEL:

NAME OF OWNER:

PHONE NO: | LICENSE NO:

EMAIL:

NAME OF CAPTAIN:

SIGNATURE & DATE:

GENERAL CHECKLIST

		YES	NO	N/A	COMMENTS
1	ARE OPERATING INSTRUCTIONS PROVIDED WITH IMO SYMBOLS?				
2	ARE FIRE DRILLS BEING HELD AS REQUIRED?				
3	ARE OFFICERS FAMILIAR WITH EMERGENCY STEERING GEAR?				
4					
5					
6					
7					
8					
9					
10					

LIFESAVING EQUIPMENT CHECKLIST

		YES	NO	N/A	COMMENTS
1	ARE SIDE BENCHES IN GOOD CONDITION?				
2	IS LIFEBOAT STERN FRAME IN GOOD CONDITION?				
3	ARE LIFEBOATS BILGES CLEAN?				
4	IS LIFEBOAT ENGINE IN GOOD CONDITION?				
5	ARE LIFEBOAT OARS IN GOOD CONDITION?				
6	ARE LIFEBOATS CORRECTLY STOWED IN DAVIT?				
7	HAVE DAVIT LIMIT SWITCHES BEEN TESTED?				
8					
9					
10					

FIRE FIGHTING CHECKLIST

		YES	NO	N/A	COMMENTS
1	IS THE MAIN FIRE LINE IN GOOD CONDITION?				
2	ARE A REQUIRED NUMBER OF PORTABLE FIRE EXTINGUISHERS AVAILABLE?				
3	ARE FIRE DAMPERS AND DOORS IN GOOD CONDITION?				
4	ARE FIRE ALARM AND DETECTION SYSTEMS WORKING WELL?				
5	ARE BREATHING APPARATUS IN GOOD CONDITION?				
6					
7					
8					
9					
10					

LOAD LINE CHECKLIST

		YES	NO	N/A	COMMENTS
1	ARE VENTILATORS TOGETHER WITH CLOSING APPLIANCES IN GOOD CONDITION?				
2	IS HULL FREE OF DAMAGES?				
3	ARE DRAUGHT MARKS VISIBLE?				
4	ARE AIR PIPES IN GOOD CONDITION?				
5	ARE COAMINGS AND HATCH COVERS CHECKED?				
6					
7					
8					
9					
10					

NOTES

SHIP MAINTENANCE CHECKLIST

NAME OF SHIP:

MAKE:	MODEL:

NAME OF OWNER:

PHONE NO:	LICENSE NO:

EMAIL:

NAME OF CAPTAIN:

SIGNATURE & DATE:

GENERAL CHECKLIST

		YES	NO	N/A	COMMENTS
1	ARE OPERATING INSTRUCTIONS PROVIDED WITH IMO SYMBOLS?				
2	ARE FIRE DRILLS BEING HELD AS REQUIRED?				
3	ARE OFFICERS FAMILIAR WITH EMERGENCY STEERING GEAR?				
4					
5					
6					
7					
8					
9					
10					

LIFESAVING EQUIPMENT CHECKLIST

		YES	NO	N/A	COMMENTS
1	ARE SIDE BENCHES IN GOOD CONDITION?				
2	IS LIFEBOAT STERN FRAME IN GOOD CONDITION?				
3	ARE LIFEBOATS BILGES CLEAN?				
4	IS LIFEBOAT ENGINE IN GOOD CONDITION?				
5	ARE LIFEBOAT OARS IN GOOD CONDITION?				
6	ARE LIFEBOATS CORRECTLY STOWED IN DAVIT?				
7	HAVE DAVIT LIMIT SWITCHES BEEN TESTED?				
8					
9					
10					

FIRE FIGHTING CHECKLIST

		YES	NO	N/A	COMMENTS
1	IS THE MAIN FIRE LINE IN GOOD CONDITION?				
2	ARE A REQUIRED NUMBER OF PORTABLE FIRE EXTINGUISHERS AVAILABLE?				
3	ARE FIRE DAMPERS AND DOORS IN GOOD CONDITION?				
4	ARE FIRE ALARM AND DETECTION SYSTEMS WORKING WELL?				
5	ARE BREATHING APPARATUS IN GOOD CONDITION?				
6					
7					
8					
9					
10					

LOAD LINE CHECKLIST

		YES	NO	N/A	COMMENTS
1	ARE VENTILATORS TOGETHER WITH CLOSING APPLIANCES IN GOOD CONDITION?				
2	IS HULL FREE OF DAMAGES?				
3	ARE DRAUGHT MARKS VISIBLE?				
4	ARE AIR PIPES IN GOOD CONDITION?				
5	ARE COAMINGS AND HATCH COVERS CHECKED?				
6					
7					
8					
9					
10					

NOTES

SHIP MAINTENANCE CHECKLIST

NAME OF SHIP:

MAKE: | MODEL:

NAME OF OWNER:

PHONE NO: | LICENSE NO:

EMAIL:

NAME OF CAPTAIN:

SIGNATURE & DATE:

GENERAL CHECKLIST

		YES	NO	N/A	COMMENTS
1	ARE OPERATING INSTRUCTIONS PROVIDED WITH IMO SYMBOLS?				
2	ARE FIRE DRILLS BEING HELD AS REQUIRED?				
3	ARE OFFICERS FAMILIAR WITH EMERGENCY STEERING GEAR?				
4					
5					
6					
7					
8					
9					
10					

LIFESAVING EQUIPMENT CHECKLIST

		YES	NO	N/A	COMMENTS
1	ARE SIDE BENCHES IN GOOD CONDITION?				
2	IS LIFEBOAT STERN FRAME IN GOOD CONDITION?				
3	ARE LIFEBOATS BILGES CLEAN?				
4	IS LIFEBOAT ENGINE IN GOOD CONDITION?				
5	ARE LIFEBOAT OARS IN GOOD CONDITION?				
6	ARE LIFEBOATS CORRECTLY STOWED IN DAVIT?				
7	HAVE DAVIT LIMIT SWITCHES BEEN TESTED?				
8					
9					
10					

FIRE FIGHTING CHECKLIST

		YES	NO	N/A	COMMENTS
1	IS THE MAIN FIRE LINE IN GOOD CONDITION?				
2	ARE A REQUIRED NUMBER OF PORTABLE FIRE EXTINGUISHERS AVAILABLE?				
3	ARE FIRE DAMPERS AND DOORS IN GOOD CONDITION?				
4	ARE FIRE ALARM AND DETECTION SYSTEMS WORKING WELL?				
5	ARE BREATHING APPARATUS IN GOOD CONDITION?				
6					
7					
8					
9					
10					

LOAD LINE CHECKLIST

		YES	NO	N/A	COMMENTS
1	ARE VENTILATORS TOGETHER WITH CLOSING APPLIANCES IN GOOD CONDITION?				
2	IS HULL FREE OF DAMAGES?				
3	ARE DRAUGHT MARKS VISIBLE?				
4	ARE AIR PIPES IN GOOD CONDITION?				
5	ARE COAMINGS AND HATCH COVERS CHECKED?				
6					
7					
8					
9					
10					

NOTES

SHIP MAINTENANCE CHECKLIST

NAME OF SHIP:	
MAKE:	MODEL:
NAME OF OWNER:	
PHONE NO:	LICENSE NO:
EMAIL:	
NAME OF CAPTAIN:	
SIGNATURE & DATE:	

GENERAL CHECKLIST

		YES	NO	N/A	COMMENTS
1	ARE OPERATING INSTRUCTIONS PROVIDED WITH IMO SYMBOLS?				
2	ARE FIRE DRILLS BEING HELD AS REQUIRED?				
3	ARE OFFICERS FAMILIAR WITH EMERGENCY STEERING GEAR?				
4					
5					
6					
7					
8					
9					
10					

LIFESAVING EQUIPMENT CHECKLIST

		YES	NO	N/A	COMMENTS
1	ARE SIDE BENCHES IN GOOD CONDITION?				
2	IS LIFEBOAT STERN FRAME IN GOOD CONDITION?				
3	ARE LIFEBOATS BILGES CLEAN?				
4	IS LIFEBOAT ENGINE IN GOOD CONDITION?				
5	ARE LIFEBOAT OARS IN GOOD CONDITION?				
6	ARE LIFEBOATS CORRECTLY STOWED IN DAVIT?				
7	HAVE DAVIT LIMIT SWITCHES BEEN TESTED?				
8					
9					
10					

FIRE FIGHTING CHECKLIST

		YES	NO	N/A	COMMENTS
1	IS THE MAIN FIRE LINE IN GOOD CONDITION?				
2	ARE A REQUIRED NUMBER OF PORTABLE FIRE EXTINGUISHERS AVAILABLE?				
3	ARE FIRE DAMPERS AND DOORS IN GOOD CONDITION?				
4	ARE FIRE ALARM AND DETECTION SYSTEMS WORKING WELL?				
5	ARE BREATHING APPARATUS IN GOOD CONDITION?				
6					
7					
8					
9					
10					

LOAD LINE CHECKLIST

		YES	NO	N/A	COMMENTS
1	ARE VENTILATORS TOGETHER WITH CLOSING APPLIANCES IN GOOD CONDITION?				
2	IS HULL FREE OF DAMAGES?				
3	ARE DRAUGHT MARKS VISIBLE?				
4	ARE AIR PIPES IN GOOD CONDITION?				
5	ARE COAMINGS AND HATCH COVERS CHECKED?				
6					
7					
8					
9					
10					

NOTES

SHIP MAINTENANCE CHECKLIST

NAME OF SHIP:	
MAKE:	MODEL:
NAME OF OWNER:	
PHONE NO:	LICENSE NO:
EMAIL:	
NAME OF CAPTAIN:	
SIGNATURE & DATE:	

GENERAL CHECKLIST

		YES	NO	N/A	COMMENTS
1	ARE OPERATING INSTRUCTIONS PROVIDED WITH IMO SYMBOLS?				
2	ARE FIRE DRILLS BEING HELD AS REQUIRED?				
3	ARE OFFICERS FAMILIAR WITH EMERGENCY STEERING GEAR?				
4					
5					
6					
7					
8					
9					
10					

LIFESAVING EQUIPMENT CHECKLIST

		YES	NO	N/A	COMMENTS
1	ARE SIDE BENCHES IN GOOD CONDITION?				
2	IS LIFEBOAT STERN FRAME IN GOOD CONDITION?				
3	ARE LIFEBOATS BILGES CLEAN?				
4	IS LIFEBOAT ENGINE IN GOOD CONDITION?				
5	ARE LIFEBOAT OARS IN GOOD CONDITION?				
6	ARE LIFEBOATS CORRECTLY STOWED IN DAVIT?				
7	HAVE DAVIT LIMIT SWITCHES BEEN TESTED?				
8					
9					
10					

FIRE FIGHTING CHECKLIST

		YES	NO	N/A	COMMENTS
1	IS THE MAIN FIRE LINE IN GOOD CONDITION?				
2	ARE A REQUIRED NUMBER OF PORTABLE FIRE EXTINGUISHERS AVAILABLE?				
3	ARE FIRE DAMPERS AND DOORS IN GOOD CONDITION?				
4	ARE FIRE ALARM AND DETECTION SYSTEMS WORKING WELL?				
5	ARE BREATHING APPARATUS IN GOOD CONDITION?				
6					
7					
8					
9					
10					

LOAD LINE CHECKLIST

		YES	NO	N/A	COMMENTS
1	ARE VENTILATORS TOGETHER WITH CLOSING APPLIANCES IN GOOD CONDITION?				
2	IS HULL FREE OF DAMAGES?				
3	ARE DRAUGHT MARKS VISIBLE?				
4	ARE AIR PIPES IN GOOD CONDITION?				
5	ARE COAMINGS AND HATCH COVERS CHECKED?				
6					
7					
8					
9					
10					

NOTES

SHIP MAINTENANCE CHECKLIST

NAME OF SHIP:	

MAKE:		MODEL:	

NAME OF OWNER:	

PHONE NO:		LICENSE NO:	

EMAIL:	

NAME OF CAPTAIN:	

SIGNATURE & DATE:	

GENERAL CHECKLIST

		YES	NO	N/A	COMMENTS
1	ARE OPERATING INSTRUCTIONS PROVIDED WITH IMO SYMBOLS?				
2	ARE FIRE DRILLS BEING HELD AS REQUIRED?				
3	ARE OFFICERS FAMILIAR WITH EMERGENCY STEERING GEAR?				
4					
5					
6					
7					
8					
9					
10					

LIFESAVING EQUIPMENT CHECKLIST

		YES	NO	N/A	COMMENTS
1	ARE SIDE BENCHES IN GOOD CONDITION?				
2	IS LIFEBOAT STERN FRAME IN GOOD CONDITION?				
3	ARE LIFEBOATS BILGES CLEAN?				
4	IS LIFEBOAT ENGINE IN GOOD CONDITION?				
5	ARE LIFEBOAT OARS IN GOOD CONDITION?				
6	ARE LIFEBOATS CORRECTLY STOWED IN DAVIT?				
7	HAVE DAVIT LIMIT SWITCHES BEEN TESTED?				
8					
9					
10					

FIRE FIGHTING CHECKLIST

		YES	NO	N/A	COMMENTS
1	IS THE MAIN FIRE LINE IN GOOD CONDITION?				
2	ARE A REQUIRED NUMBER OF PORTABLE FIRE EXTINGUISHERS AVAILABLE?				
3	ARE FIRE DAMPERS AND DOORS IN GOOD CONDITION?				
4	ARE FIRE ALARM AND DETECTION SYSTEMS WORKING WELL?				
5	ARE BREATHING APPARATUS IN GOOD CONDITION?				
6					
7					
8					
9					
10					

LOAD LINE CHECKLIST

		YES	NO	N/A	COMMENTS
1	ARE VENTILATORS TOGETHER WITH CLOSING APPLIANCES IN GOOD CONDITION?				
2	IS HULL FREE OF DAMAGES?				
3	ARE DRAUGHT MARKS VISIBLE?				
4	ARE AIR PIPES IN GOOD CONDITION?				
5	ARE COAMINGS AND HATCH COVERS CHECKED?				
6					
7					
8					
9					
10					

NOTES

SHIP MAINTENANCE CHECKLIST

NAME OF SHIP:	

MAKE:	MODEL:

NAME OF OWNER:

PHONE NO:	LICENSE NO:

EMAIL:

NAME OF CAPTAIN:

SIGNATURE & DATE:

GENERAL CHECKLIST

		YES	NO	N/A	COMMENTS
1	ARE OPERATING INSTRUCTIONS PROVIDED WITH IMO SYMBOLS?				
2	ARE FIRE DRILLS BEING HELD AS REQUIRED?				
3	ARE OFFICERS FAMILIAR WITH EMERGENCY STEERING GEAR?				
4					
5					
6					
7					
8					
9					
10					

LIFESAVING EQUIPMENT CHECKLIST

		YES	NO	N/A	COMMENTS
1	ARE SIDE BENCHES IN GOOD CONDITION?				
2	IS LIFEBOAT STERN FRAME IN GOOD CONDITION?				
3	ARE LIFEBOATS BILGES CLEAN?				
4	IS LIFEBOAT ENGINE IN GOOD CONDITION?				
5	ARE LIFEBOAT OARS IN GOOD CONDITION?				
6	ARE LIFEBOATS CORRECTLY STOWED IN DAVIT?				
7	HAVE DAVIT LIMIT SWITCHES BEEN TESTED?				
8					
9					
10					

FIRE FIGHTING CHECKLIST

		YES	NO	N/A	COMMENTS
1	IS THE MAIN FIRE LINE IN GOOD CONDITION?				
2	ARE A REQUIRED NUMBER OF PORTABLE FIRE EXTINGUISHERS AVAILABLE?				
3	ARE FIRE DAMPERS AND DOORS IN GOOD CONDITION?				
4	ARE FIRE ALARM AND DETECTION SYSTEMS WORKING WELL?				
5	ARE BREATHING APPARATUS IN GOOD CONDITION?				
6					
7					
8					
9					
10					

LOAD LINE CHECKLIST

		YES	NO	N/A	COMMENTS
1	ARE VENTILATORS TOGETHER WITH CLOSING APPLIANCES IN GOOD CONDITION?				
2	IS HULL FREE OF DAMAGES?				
3	ARE DRAUGHT MARKS VISIBLE?				
4	ARE AIR PIPES IN GOOD CONDITION?				
5	ARE COAMINGS AND HATCH COVERS CHECKED?				
6					
7					
8					
9					
10					

NOTES

SHIP MAINTENANCE CHECKLIST

NAME OF SHIP:

MAKE: | MODEL:

NAME OF OWNER:

PHONE NO: | LICENSE NO:

EMAIL:

NAME OF CAPTAIN:

SIGNATURE & DATE:

GENERAL CHECKLIST

		YES	NO	N/A	COMMENTS
1	ARE OPERATING INSTRUCTIONS PROVIDED WITH IMO SYMBOLS?				
2	ARE FIRE DRILLS BEING HELD AS REQUIRED?				
3	ARE OFFICERS FAMILIAR WITH EMERGENCY STEERING GEAR?				
4					
5					
6					
7					
8					
9					
10					

LIFESAVING EQUIPMENT CHECKLIST

		YES	NO	N/A	COMMENTS
1	ARE SIDE BENCHES IN GOOD CONDITION?				
2	IS LIFEBOAT STERN FRAME IN GOOD CONDITION?				
3	ARE LIFEBOATS BILGES CLEAN?				
4	IS LIFEBOAT ENGINE IN GOOD CONDITION?				
5	ARE LIFEBOAT OARS IN GOOD CONDITION?				
6	ARE LIFEBOATS CORRECTLY STOWED IN DAVIT?				
7	HAVE DAVIT LIMIT SWITCHES BEEN TESTED?				
8					
9					
10					

FIRE FIGHTING CHECKLIST

		YES	NO	N/A	COMMENTS
1	IS THE MAIN FIRE LINE IN GOOD CONDITION?				
2	ARE A REQUIRED NUMBER OF PORTABLE FIRE EXTINGUISHERS AVAILABLE?				
3	ARE FIRE DAMPERS AND DOORS IN GOOD CONDITION?				
4	ARE FIRE ALARM AND DETECTION SYSTEMS WORKING WELL?				
5	ARE BREATHING APPARATUS IN GOOD CONDITION?				
6					
7					
8					
9					
10					

LOAD LINE CHECKLIST

		YES	NO	N/A	COMMENTS
1	ARE VENTILATORS TOGETHER WITH CLOSING APPLIANCES IN GOOD CONDITION?				
2	IS HULL FREE OF DAMAGES?				
3	ARE DRAUGHT MARKS VISIBLE?				
4	ARE AIR PIPES IN GOOD CONDITION?				
5	ARE COAMINGS AND HATCH COVERS CHECKED?				
6					
7					
8					
9					
10					

NOTES

SHIP MAINTENANCE CHECKLIST

NAME OF SHIP:	
MAKE:	MODEL:
NAME OF OWNER:	
PHONE NO:	LICENSE NO:
EMAIL:	
NAME OF CAPTAIN:	
SIGNATURE & DATE:	

GENERAL CHECKLIST

		YES	NO	N/A	COMMENTS
1	ARE OPERATING INSTRUCTIONS PROVIDED WITH IMO SYMBOLS?				
2	ARE FIRE DRILLS BEING HELD AS REQUIRED?				
3	ARE OFFICERS FAMILIAR WITH EMERGENCY STEERING GEAR?				
4					
5					
6					
7					
8					
9					
10					

LIFESAVING EQUIPMENT CHECKLIST

		YES	NO	N/A	COMMENTS
1	ARE SIDE BENCHES IN GOOD CONDITION?				
2	IS LIFEBOAT STERN FRAME IN GOOD CONDITION?				
3	ARE LIFEBOATS BILGES CLEAN?				
4	IS LIFEBOAT ENGINE IN GOOD CONDITION?				
5	ARE LIFEBOAT OARS IN GOOD CONDITION?				
6	ARE LIFEBOATS CORRECTLY STOWED IN DAVIT?				
7	HAVE DAVIT LIMIT SWITCHES BEEN TESTED?				
8					
9					
10					

FIRE FIGHTING CHECKLIST

		YES	NO	N/A	COMMENTS
1	IS THE MAIN FIRE LINE IN GOOD CONDITION?				
2	ARE A REQUIRED NUMBER OF PORTABLE FIRE EXTINGUISHERS AVAILABLE?				
3	ARE FIRE DAMPERS AND DOORS IN GOOD CONDITION?				
4	ARE FIRE ALARM AND DETECTION SYSTEMS WORKING WELL?				
5	ARE BREATHING APPARATUS IN GOOD CONDITION?				
6					
7					
8					
9					
10					

LOAD LINE CHECKLIST

		YES	NO	N/A	COMMENTS
1	ARE VENTILATORS TOGETHER WITH CLOSING APPLIANCES IN GOOD CONDITION?				
2	IS HULL FREE OF DAMAGES?				
3	ARE DRAUGHT MARKS VISIBLE?				
4	ARE AIR PIPES IN GOOD CONDITION?				
5	ARE COAMINGS AND HATCH COVERS CHECKED?				
6					
7					
8					
9					
10					

NOTES

SHIP MAINTENANCE CHECKLIST

NAME OF SHIP:	
MAKE:	MODEL:
NAME OF OWNER:	
PHONE NO:	LICENSE NO:
EMAIL:	
NAME OF CAPTAIN:	
SIGNATURE & DATE:	

GENERAL CHECKLIST

		YES	NO	N/A	COMMENTS
1	ARE OPERATING INSTRUCTIONS PROVIDED WITH IMO SYMBOLS?				
2	ARE FIRE DRILLS BEING HELD AS REQUIRED?				
3	ARE OFFICERS FAMILIAR WITH EMERGENCY STEERING GEAR?				
4					
5					
6					
7					
8					
9					
10					

LIFESAVING EQUIPMENT CHECKLIST

		YES	NO	N/A	COMMENTS
1	ARE SIDE BENCHES IN GOOD CONDITION?				
2	IS LIFEBOAT STERN FRAME IN GOOD CONDITION?				
3	ARE LIFEBOATS BILGES CLEAN?				
4	IS LIFEBOAT ENGINE IN GOOD CONDITION?				
5	ARE LIFEBOAT OARS IN GOOD CONDITION?				
6	ARE LIFEBOATS CORRECTLY STOWED IN DAVIT?				
7	HAVE DAVIT LIMIT SWITCHES BEEN TESTED?				
8					
9					
10					

FIRE FIGHTING CHECKLIST

		YES	NO	N/A	COMMENTS
1	IS THE MAIN FIRE LINE IN GOOD CONDITION?				
2	ARE A REQUIRED NUMBER OF PORTABLE FIRE EXTINGUISHERS AVAILABLE?				
3	ARE FIRE DAMPERS AND DOORS IN GOOD CONDITION?				
4	ARE FIRE ALARM AND DETECTION SYSTEMS WORKING WELL?				
5	ARE BREATHING APPARATUS IN GOOD CONDITION?				
6					
7					
8					
9					
10					

LOAD LINE CHECKLIST

		YES	NO	N/A	COMMENTS
1	ARE VENTILATORS TOGETHER WITH CLOSING APPLIANCES IN GOOD CONDITION?				
2	IS HULL FREE OF DAMAGES?				
3	ARE DRAUGHT MARKS VISIBLE?				
4	ARE AIR PIPES IN GOOD CONDITION?				
5	ARE COAMINGS AND HATCH COVERS CHECKED?				
6					
7					
8					
9					
10					

NOTES

SHIP MAINTENANCE CHECKLIST

NAME OF SHIP:	
MAKE:	MODEL:
NAME OF OWNER:	
PHONE NO:	LICENSE NO:
EMAIL:	
NAME OF CAPTAIN:	
SIGNATURE & DATE:	

GENERAL CHECKLIST

		YES	NO	N/A	COMMENTS
1	ARE OPERATING INSTRUCTIONS PROVIDED WITH IMO SYMBOLS?				
2	ARE FIRE DRILLS BEING HELD AS REQUIRED?				
3	ARE OFFICERS FAMILIAR WITH EMERGENCY STEERING GEAR?				
4					
5					
6					
7					
8					
9					
10					

LIFESAVING EQUIPMENT CHECKLIST

		YES	NO	N/A	COMMENTS
1	ARE SIDE BENCHES IN GOOD CONDITION?				
2	IS LIFEBOAT STERN FRAME IN GOOD CONDITION?				
3	ARE LIFEBOATS BILGES CLEAN?				
4	IS LIFEBOAT ENGINE IN GOOD CONDITION?				
5	ARE LIFEBOAT OARS IN GOOD CONDITION?				
6	ARE LIFEBOATS CORRECTLY STOWED IN DAVIT?				
7	HAVE DAVIT LIMIT SWITCHES BEEN TESTED?				
8					
9					
10					

FIRE FIGHTING CHECKLIST

		YES	NO	N/A	COMMENTS
1	IS THE MAIN FIRE LINE IN GOOD CONDITION?				
2	ARE A REQUIRED NUMBER OF PORTABLE FIRE EXTINGUISHERS AVAILABLE?				
3	ARE FIRE DAMPERS AND DOORS IN GOOD CONDITION?				
4	ARE FIRE ALARM AND DETECTION SYSTEMS WORKING WELL?				
5	ARE BREATHING APPARATUS IN GOOD CONDITION?				
6					
7					
8					
9					
10					

LOAD LINE CHECKLIST

		YES	NO	N/A	COMMENTS
1	ARE VENTILATORS TOGETHER WITH CLOSING APPLIANCES IN GOOD CONDITION?				
2	IS HULL FREE OF DAMAGES?				
3	ARE DRAUGHT MARKS VISIBLE?				
4	ARE AIR PIPES IN GOOD CONDITION?				
5	ARE COAMINGS AND HATCH COVERS CHECKED?				
6					
7					
8					
9					
10					

NOTES

SHIP MAINTENANCE CHECKLIST

NAME OF SHIP:	
MAKE:	MODEL:
NAME OF OWNER:	
PHONE NO:	LICENSE NO:
EMAIL:	
NAME OF CAPTAIN:	
SIGNATURE & DATE:	

GENERAL CHECKLIST

		YES	NO	N/A	COMMENTS
1	ARE OPERATING INSTRUCTIONS PROVIDED WITH IMO SYMBOLS?				
2	ARE FIRE DRILLS BEING HELD AS REQUIRED?				
3	ARE OFFICERS FAMILIAR WITH EMERGENCY STEERING GEAR?				
4					
5					
6					
7					
8					
9					
10					

LIFESAVING EQUIPMENT CHECKLIST

		YES	NO	N/A	COMMENTS
1	ARE SIDE BENCHES IN GOOD CONDITION?				
2	IS LIFEBOAT STERN FRAME IN GOOD CONDITION?				
3	ARE LIFEBOATS BILGES CLEAN?				
4	IS LIFEBOAT ENGINE IN GOOD CONDITION?				
5	ARE LIFEBOAT OARS IN GOOD CONDITION?				
6	ARE LIFEBOATS CORRECTLY STOWED IN DAVIT?				
7	HAVE DAVIT LIMIT SWITCHES BEEN TESTED?				
8					
9					
10					

FIRE FIGHTING CHECKLIST

		YES	NO	N/A	COMMENTS
1	IS THE MAIN FIRE LINE IN GOOD CONDITION?				
2	ARE A REQUIRED NUMBER OF PORTABLE FIRE EXTINGUISHERS AVAILABLE?				
3	ARE FIRE DAMPERS AND DOORS IN GOOD CONDITION?				
4	ARE FIRE ALARM AND DETECTION SYSTEMS WORKING WELL?				
5	ARE BREATHING APPARATUS IN GOOD CONDITION?				
6					
7					
8					
9					
10					

LOAD LINE CHECKLIST

		YES	NO	N/A	COMMENTS
1	ARE VENTILATORS TOGETHER WITH CLOSING APPLIANCES IN GOOD CONDITION?				
2	IS HULL FREE OF DAMAGES?				
3	ARE DRAUGHT MARKS VISIBLE?				
4	ARE AIR PIPES IN GOOD CONDITION?				
5	ARE COAMINGS AND HATCH COVERS CHECKED?				
6					
7					
8					
9					
10					

NOTES

SHIP MAINTENANCE CHECKLIST

NAME OF SHIP:

MAKE: MODEL:

NAME OF OWNER:

PHONE NO: LICENSE NO:

EMAIL:

NAME OF CAPTAIN:

SIGNATURE & DATE:

GENERAL CHECKLIST

		YES	NO	N/A	COMMENTS
1	ARE OPERATING INSTRUCTIONS PROVIDED WITH IMO SYMBOLS?				
2	ARE FIRE DRILLS BEING HELD AS REQUIRED?				
3	ARE OFFICERS FAMILIAR WITH EMERGENCY STEERING GEAR?				
4					
5					
6					
7					
8					
9					
10					

LIFESAVING EQUIPMENT CHECKLIST

		YES	NO	N/A	COMMENTS
1	ARE SIDE BENCHES IN GOOD CONDITION?				
2	IS LIFEBOAT STERN FRAME IN GOOD CONDITION?				
3	ARE LIFEBOATS BILGES CLEAN?				
4	IS LIFEBOAT ENGINE IN GOOD CONDITION?				
5	ARE LIFEBOAT OARS IN GOOD CONDITION?				
6	ARE LIFEBOATS CORRECTLY STOWED IN DAVIT?				
7	HAVE DAVIT LIMIT SWITCHES BEEN TESTED?				
8					
9					
10					

FIRE FIGHTING CHECKLIST

		YES	NO	N/A	COMMENTS
1	IS THE MAIN FIRE LINE IN GOOD CONDITION?				
2	ARE A REQUIRED NUMBER OF PORTABLE FIRE EXTINGUISHERS AVAILABLE?				
3	ARE FIRE DAMPERS AND DOORS IN GOOD CONDITION?				
4	ARE FIRE ALARM AND DETECTION SYSTEMS WORKING WELL?				
5	ARE BREATHING APPARATUS IN GOOD CONDITION?				
6					
7					
8					
9					
10					

LOAD LINE CHECKLIST

		YES	NO	N/A	COMMENTS
1	ARE VENTILATORS TOGETHER WITH CLOSING APPLIANCES IN GOOD CONDITION?				
2	IS HULL FREE OF DAMAGES?				
3	ARE DRAUGHT MARKS VISIBLE?				
4	ARE AIR PIPES IN GOOD CONDITION?				
5	ARE COAMINGS AND HATCH COVERS CHECKED?				
6					
7					
8					
9					
10					

NOTES

SHIP MAINTENANCE CHECKLIST

NAME OF SHIP:

MAKE: | MODEL:

NAME OF OWNER:

PHONE NO: | LICENSE NO:

EMAIL:

NAME OF CAPTAIN:

SIGNATURE & DATE:

GENERAL CHECKLIST

		YES	NO	N/A	COMMENTS
1	ARE OPERATING INSTRUCTIONS PROVIDED WITH IMO SYMBOLS?				
2	ARE FIRE DRILLS BEING HELD AS REQUIRED?				
3	ARE OFFICERS FAMILIAR WITH EMERGENCY STEERING GEAR?				
4					
5					
6					
7					
8					
9					
10					

LIFESAVING EQUIPMENT CHECKLIST

		YES	NO	N/A	COMMENTS
1	ARE SIDE BENCHES IN GOOD CONDITION?				
2	IS LIFEBOAT STERN FRAME IN GOOD CONDITION?				
3	ARE LIFEBOATS BILGES CLEAN?				
4	IS LIFEBOAT ENGINE IN GOOD CONDITION?				
5	ARE LIFEBOAT OARS IN GOOD CONDITION?				
6	ARE LIFEBOATS CORRECTLY STOWED IN DAVIT?				
7	HAVE DAVIT LIMIT SWITCHES BEEN TESTED?				
8					
9					
10					

FIRE FIGHTING CHECKLIST

		YES	NO	N/A	COMMENTS
1	IS THE MAIN FIRE LINE IN GOOD CONDITION?				
2	ARE A REQUIRED NUMBER OF PORTABLE FIRE EXTINGUISHERS AVAILABLE?				
3	ARE FIRE DAMPERS AND DOORS IN GOOD CONDITION?				
4	ARE FIRE ALARM AND DETECTION SYSTEMS WORKING WELL?				
5	ARE BREATHING APPARATUS IN GOOD CONDITION?				
6					
7					
8					
9					
10					

LOAD LINE CHECKLIST

		YES	NO	N/A	COMMENTS
1	ARE VENTILATORS TOGETHER WITH CLOSING APPLIANCES IN GOOD CONDITION?				
2	IS HULL FREE OF DAMAGES?				
3	ARE DRAUGHT MARKS VISIBLE?				
4	ARE AIR PIPES IN GOOD CONDITION?				
5	ARE COAMINGS AND HATCH COVERS CHECKED?				
6					
7					
8					
9					
10					

NOTES

SHIP MAINTENANCE CHECKLIST

NAME OF SHIP:	
MAKE:	MODEL:
NAME OF OWNER:	
PHONE NO:	LICENSE NO:
EMAIL:	
NAME OF CAPTAIN:	
SIGNATURE & DATE:	

GENERAL CHECKLIST

		YES	NO	N/A	COMMENTS
1	ARE OPERATING INSTRUCTIONS PROVIDED WITH IMO SYMBOLS?				
2	ARE FIRE DRILLS BEING HELD AS REQUIRED?				
3	ARE OFFICERS FAMILIAR WITH EMERGENCY STEERING GEAR?				
4					
5					
6					
7					
8					
9					
10					

LIFESAVING EQUIPMENT CHECKLIST

		YES	NO	N/A	COMMENTS
1	ARE SIDE BENCHES IN GOOD CONDITION?				
2	IS LIFEBOAT STERN FRAME IN GOOD CONDITION?				
3	ARE LIFEBOATS BILGES CLEAN?				
4	IS LIFEBOAT ENGINE IN GOOD CONDITION?				
5	ARE LIFEBOAT OARS IN GOOD CONDITION?				
6	ARE LIFEBOATS CORRECTLY STOWED IN DAVIT?				
7	HAVE DAVIT LIMIT SWITCHES BEEN TESTED?				
8					
9					
10					

FIRE FIGHTING CHECKLIST

		YES	NO	N/A	COMMENTS
1	IS THE MAIN FIRE LINE IN GOOD CONDITION?				
2	ARE A REQUIRED NUMBER OF PORTABLE FIRE EXTINGUISHERS AVAILABLE?				
3	ARE FIRE DAMPERS AND DOORS IN GOOD CONDITION?				
4	ARE FIRE ALARM AND DETECTION SYSTEMS WORKING WELL?				
5	ARE BREATHING APPARATUS IN GOOD CONDITION?				
6					
7					
8					
9					
10					

LOAD LINE CHECKLIST

		YES	NO	N/A	COMMENTS
1	ARE VENTILATORS TOGETHER WITH CLOSING APPLIANCES IN GOOD CONDITION?				
2	IS HULL FREE OF DAMAGES?				
3	ARE DRAUGHT MARKS VISIBLE?				
4	ARE AIR PIPES IN GOOD CONDITION?				
5	ARE COAMINGS AND HATCH COVERS CHECKED?				
6					
7					
8					
9					
10					

NOTES

SHIP MAINTENANCE CHECKLIST

NAME OF SHIP:	
MAKE:	MODEL:
NAME OF OWNER:	
PHONE NO:	LICENSE NO:
EMAIL:	
NAME OF CAPTAIN:	
SIGNATURE & DATE:	

GENERAL CHECKLIST

		YES	NO	N/A	COMMENTS
1	ARE OPERATING INSTRUCTIONS PROVIDED WITH IMO SYMBOLS?				
2	ARE FIRE DRILLS BEING HELD AS REQUIRED?				
3	ARE OFFICERS FAMILIAR WITH EMERGENCY STEERING GEAR?				
4					
5					
6					
7					
8					
9					
10					

LIFESAVING EQUIPMENT CHECKLIST

		YES	NO	N/A	COMMENTS
1	ARE SIDE BENCHES IN GOOD CONDITION?				
2	IS LIFEBOAT STERN FRAME IN GOOD CONDITION?				
3	ARE LIFEBOATS BILGES CLEAN?				
4	IS LIFEBOAT ENGINE IN GOOD CONDITION?				
5	ARE LIFEBOAT OARS IN GOOD CONDITION?				
6	ARE LIFEBOATS CORRECTLY STOWED IN DAVIT?				
7	HAVE DAVIT LIMIT SWITCHES BEEN TESTED?				
8					
9					
10					

FIRE FIGHTING CHECKLIST

		YES	NO	N/A	COMMENTS
1	IS THE MAIN FIRE LINE IN GOOD CONDITION?				
2	ARE A REQUIRED NUMBER OF PORTABLE FIRE EXTINGUISHERS AVAILABLE?				
3	ARE FIRE DAMPERS AND DOORS IN GOOD CONDITION?				
4	ARE FIRE ALARM AND DETECTION SYSTEMS WORKING WELL?				
5	ARE BREATHING APPARATUS IN GOOD CONDITION?				
6					
7					
8					
9					
10					

LOAD LINE CHECKLIST

		YES	NO	N/A	COMMENTS
1	ARE VENTILATORS TOGETHER WITH CLOSING APPLIANCES IN GOOD CONDITION?				
2	IS HULL FREE OF DAMAGES?				
3	ARE DRAUGHT MARKS VISIBLE?				
4	ARE AIR PIPES IN GOOD CONDITION?				
5	ARE COAMINGS AND HATCH COVERS CHECKED?				
6					
7					
8					
9					
10					

NOTES

SHIP MAINTENANCE CHECKLIST

NAME OF SHIP:

MAKE: | MODEL:

NAME OF OWNER:

PHONE NO: | LICENSE NO:

EMAIL:

NAME OF CAPTAIN:

SIGNATURE & DATE:

GENERAL CHECKLIST

		YES	NO	N/A	COMMENTS
1	ARE OPERATING INSTRUCTIONS PROVIDED WITH IMO SYMBOLS?				
2	ARE FIRE DRILLS BEING HELD AS REQUIRED?				
3	ARE OFFICERS FAMILIAR WITH EMERGENCY STEERING GEAR?				
4					
5					
6					
7					
8					
9					
10					

LIFESAVING EQUIPMENT CHECKLIST

		YES	NO	N/A	COMMENTS
1	ARE SIDE BENCHES IN GOOD CONDITION?				
2	IS LIFEBOAT STERN FRAME IN GOOD CONDITION?				
3	ARE LIFEBOATS BILGES CLEAN?				
4	IS LIFEBOAT ENGINE IN GOOD CONDITION?				
5	ARE LIFEBOAT OARS IN GOOD CONDITION?				
6	ARE LIFEBOATS CORRECTLY STOWED IN DAVIT?				
7	HAVE DAVIT LIMIT SWITCHES BEEN TESTED?				
8					
9					
10					

FIRE FIGHTING CHECKLIST

		YES	NO	N/A	COMMENTS
1	IS THE MAIN FIRE LINE IN GOOD CONDITION?				
2	ARE A REQUIRED NUMBER OF PORTABLE FIRE EXTINGUISHERS AVAILABLE?				
3	ARE FIRE DAMPERS AND DOORS IN GOOD CONDITION?				
4	ARE FIRE ALARM AND DETECTION SYSTEMS WORKING WELL?				
5	ARE BREATHING APPARATUS IN GOOD CONDITION?				
6					
7					
8					
9					
10					

LOAD LINE CHECKLIST

		YES	NO	N/A	COMMENTS
1	ARE VENTILATORS TOGETHER WITH CLOSING APPLIANCES IN GOOD CONDITION?				
2	IS HULL FREE OF DAMAGES?				
3	ARE DRAUGHT MARKS VISIBLE?				
4	ARE AIR PIPES IN GOOD CONDITION?				
5	ARE COAMINGS AND HATCH COVERS CHECKED?				
6					
7					
8					
9					
10					

NOTES

SHIP MAINTENANCE CHECKLIST

NAME OF SHIP:	
MAKE:	MODEL:
NAME OF OWNER:	
PHONE NO:	LICENSE NO:
EMAIL:	
NAME OF CAPTAIN:	
SIGNATURE & DATE:	

GENERAL CHECKLIST

		YES	NO	N/A	COMMENTS
1	ARE OPERATING INSTRUCTIONS PROVIDED WITH IMO SYMBOLS?				
2	ARE FIRE DRILLS BEING HELD AS REQUIRED?				
3	ARE OFFICERS FAMILIAR WITH EMERGENCY STEERING GEAR?				
4					
5					
6					
7					
8					
9					
10					

LIFESAVING EQUIPMENT CHECKLIST

		YES	NO	N/A	COMMENTS
1	ARE SIDE BENCHES IN GOOD CONDITION?				
2	IS LIFEBOAT STERN FRAME IN GOOD CONDITION?				
3	ARE LIFEBOATS BILGES CLEAN?				
4	IS LIFEBOAT ENGINE IN GOOD CONDITION?				
5	ARE LIFEBOAT OARS IN GOOD CONDITION?				
6	ARE LIFEBOATS CORRECTLY STOWED IN DAVIT?				
7	HAVE DAVIT LIMIT SWITCHES BEEN TESTED?				
8					
9					
10					

FIRE FIGHTING CHECKLIST

		YES	NO	N/A	COMMENTS
1	IS THE MAIN FIRE LINE IN GOOD CONDITION?				
2	ARE A REQUIRED NUMBER OF PORTABLE FIRE EXTINGUISHERS AVAILABLE?				
3	ARE FIRE DAMPERS AND DOORS IN GOOD CONDITION?				
4	ARE FIRE ALARM AND DETECTION SYSTEMS WORKING WELL?				
5	ARE BREATHING APPARATUS IN GOOD CONDITION?				
6					
7					
8					
9					
10					

LOAD LINE CHECKLIST

		YES	NO	N/A	COMMENTS
1	ARE VENTILATORS TOGETHER WITH CLOSING APPLIANCES IN GOOD CONDITION?				
2	IS HULL FREE OF DAMAGES?				
3	ARE DRAUGHT MARKS VISIBLE?				
4	ARE AIR PIPES IN GOOD CONDITION?				
5	ARE COAMINGS AND HATCH COVERS CHECKED?				
6					
7					
8					
9					
10					

NOTES

SHIP MAINTENANCE CHECKLIST

NAME OF SHIP:	
MAKE:	MODEL:
NAME OF OWNER:	
PHONE NO:	LICENSE NO:
EMAIL:	
NAME OF CAPTAIN:	
SIGNATURE & DATE:	

GENERAL CHECKLIST

		YES	NO	N/A	COMMENTS
1	ARE OPERATING INSTRUCTIONS PROVIDED WITH IMO SYMBOLS?				
2	ARE FIRE DRILLS BEING HELD AS REQUIRED?				
3	ARE OFFICERS FAMILIAR WITH EMERGENCY STEERING GEAR?				
4					
5					
6					
7					
8					
9					
10					

LIFESAVING EQUIPMENT CHECKLIST

		YES	NO	N/A	COMMENTS
1	ARE SIDE BENCHES IN GOOD CONDITION?				
2	IS LIFEBOAT STERN FRAME IN GOOD CONDITION?				
3	ARE LIFEBOATS BILGES CLEAN?				
4	IS LIFEBOAT ENGINE IN GOOD CONDITION?				
5	ARE LIFEBOAT OARS IN GOOD CONDITION?				
6	ARE LIFEBOATS CORRECTLY STOWED IN DAVIT?				
7	HAVE DAVIT LIMIT SWITCHES BEEN TESTED?				
8					
9					
10					

FIRE FIGHTING CHECKLIST

		YES	NO	N/A	COMMENTS
1	IS THE MAIN FIRE LINE IN GOOD CONDITION?				
2	ARE A REQUIRED NUMBER OF PORTABLE FIRE EXTINGUISHERS AVAILABLE?				
3	ARE FIRE DAMPERS AND DOORS IN GOOD CONDITION?				
4	ARE FIRE ALARM AND DETECTION SYSTEMS WORKING WELL?				
5	ARE BREATHING APPARATUS IN GOOD CONDITION?				
6					
7					
8					
9					
10					

LOAD LINE CHECKLIST

		YES	NO	N/A	COMMENTS
1	ARE VENTILATORS TOGETHER WITH CLOSING APPLIANCES IN GOOD CONDITION?				
2	IS HULL FREE OF DAMAGES?				
3	ARE DRAUGHT MARKS VISIBLE?				
4	ARE AIR PIPES IN GOOD CONDITION?				
5	ARE COAMINGS AND HATCH COVERS CHECKED?				
6					
7					
8					
9					
10					

NOTES

SHIP MAINTENANCE CHECKLIST

NAME OF SHIP:	
MAKE:	MODEL:
NAME OF OWNER:	
PHONE NO:	LICENSE NO:
EMAIL:	
NAME OF CAPTAIN:	
SIGNATURE & DATE:	

GENERAL CHECKLIST

		YES	NO	N/A	COMMENTS
1	ARE OPERATING INSTRUCTIONS PROVIDED WITH IMO SYMBOLS?				
2	ARE FIRE DRILLS BEING HELD AS REQUIRED?				
3	ARE OFFICERS FAMILIAR WITH EMERGENCY STEERING GEAR?				
4					
5					
6					
7					
8					
9					
10					

LIFESAVING EQUIPMENT CHECKLIST

		YES	NO	N/A	COMMENTS
1	ARE SIDE BENCHES IN GOOD CONDITION?				
2	IS LIFEBOAT STERN FRAME IN GOOD CONDITION?				
3	ARE LIFEBOATS BILGES CLEAN?				
4	IS LIFEBOAT ENGINE IN GOOD CONDITION?				
5	ARE LIFEBOAT OARS IN GOOD CONDITION?				
6	ARE LIFEBOATS CORRECTLY STOWED IN DAVIT?				
7	HAVE DAVIT LIMIT SWITCHES BEEN TESTED?				
8					
9					
10					

FIRE FIGHTING CHECKLIST

		YES	NO	N/A	COMMENTS
1	IS THE MAIN FIRE LINE IN GOOD CONDITION?				
2	ARE A REQUIRED NUMBER OF PORTABLE FIRE EXTINGUISHERS AVAILABLE?				
3	ARE FIRE DAMPERS AND DOORS IN GOOD CONDITION?				
4	ARE FIRE ALARM AND DETECTION SYSTEMS WORKING WELL?				
5	ARE BREATHING APPARATUS IN GOOD CONDITION?				
6					
7					
8					
9					
10					

LOAD LINE CHECKLIST

		YES	NO	N/A	COMMENTS
1	ARE VENTILATORS TOGETHER WITH CLOSING APPLIANCES IN GOOD CONDITION?				
2	IS HULL FREE OF DAMAGES?				
3	ARE DRAUGHT MARKS VISIBLE?				
4	ARE AIR PIPES IN GOOD CONDITION?				
5	ARE COAMINGS AND HATCH COVERS CHECKED?				
6					
7					
8					
9					
10					

NOTES

SHIP MAINTENANCE CHECKLIST

NAME OF SHIP:	
MAKE:	MODEL:
NAME OF OWNER:	
PHONE NO:	LICENSE NO:
EMAIL:	
NAME OF CAPTAIN:	
SIGNATURE & DATE:	

GENERAL CHECKLIST

		YES	NO	N/A	COMMENTS
1	ARE OPERATING INSTRUCTIONS PROVIDED WITH IMO SYMBOLS?				
2	ARE FIRE DRILLS BEING HELD AS REQUIRED?				
3	ARE OFFICERS FAMILIAR WITH EMERGENCY STEERING GEAR?				
4					
5					
6					
7					
8					
9					
10					

LIFESAVING EQUIPMENT CHECKLIST

		YES	NO	N/A	COMMENTS
1	ARE SIDE BENCHES IN GOOD CONDITION?				
2	IS LIFEBOAT STERN FRAME IN GOOD CONDITION?				
3	ARE LIFEBOATS BILGES CLEAN?				
4	IS LIFEBOAT ENGINE IN GOOD CONDITION?				
5	ARE LIFEBOAT OARS IN GOOD CONDITION?				
6	ARE LIFEBOATS CORRECTLY STOWED IN DAVIT?				
7	HAVE DAVIT LIMIT SWITCHES BEEN TESTED?				
8					
9					
10					

FIRE FIGHTING CHECKLIST

		YES	NO	N/A	COMMENTS
1	IS THE MAIN FIRE LINE IN GOOD CONDITION?				
2	ARE A REQUIRED NUMBER OF PORTABLE FIRE EXTINGUISHERS AVAILABLE?				
3	ARE FIRE DAMPERS AND DOORS IN GOOD CONDITION?				
4	ARE FIRE ALARM AND DETECTION SYSTEMS WORKING WELL?				
5	ARE BREATHING APPARATUS IN GOOD CONDITION?				
6					
7					
8					
9					
10					

LOAD LINE CHECKLIST

		YES	NO	N/A	COMMENTS
1	ARE VENTILATORS TOGETHER WITH CLOSING APPLIANCES IN GOOD CONDITION?				
2	IS HULL FREE OF DAMAGES?				
3	ARE DRAUGHT MARKS VISIBLE?				
4	ARE AIR PIPES IN GOOD CONDITION?				
5	ARE COAMINGS AND HATCH COVERS CHECKED?				
6					
7					
8					
9					
10					

NOTES

SHIP MAINTENANCE CHECKLIST

NAME OF SHIP:	
MAKE:	MODEL:
NAME OF OWNER:	
PHONE NO:	LICENSE NO:
EMAIL:	
NAME OF CAPTAIN:	
SIGNATURE & DATE:	

GENERAL CHECKLIST

		YES	NO	N/A	COMMENTS
1	ARE OPERATING INSTRUCTIONS PROVIDED WITH IMO SYMBOLS?				
2	ARE FIRE DRILLS BEING HELD AS REQUIRED?				
3	ARE OFFICERS FAMILIAR WITH EMERGENCY STEERING GEAR?				
4					
5					
6					
7					
8					
9					
10					

LIFESAVING EQUIPMENT CHECKLIST

		YES	NO	N/A	COMMENTS
1	ARE SIDE BENCHES IN GOOD CONDITION?				
2	IS LIFEBOAT STERN FRAME IN GOOD CONDITION?				
3	ARE LIFEBOATS BILGES CLEAN?				
4	IS LIFEBOAT ENGINE IN GOOD CONDITION?				
5	ARE LIFEBOAT OARS IN GOOD CONDITION?				
6	ARE LIFEBOATS CORRECTLY STOWED IN DAVIT?				
7	HAVE DAVIT LIMIT SWITCHES BEEN TESTED?				
8					
9					
10					

FIRE FIGHTING CHECKLIST

		YES	NO	N/A	COMMENTS
1	IS THE MAIN FIRE LINE IN GOOD CONDITION?				
2	ARE A REQUIRED NUMBER OF PORTABLE FIRE EXTINGUISHERS AVAILABLE?				
3	ARE FIRE DAMPERS AND DOORS IN GOOD CONDITION?				
4	ARE FIRE ALARM AND DETECTION SYSTEMS WORKING WELL?				
5	ARE BREATHING APPARATUS IN GOOD CONDITION?				
6					
7					
8					
9					
10					

LOAD LINE CHECKLIST

		YES	NO	N/A	COMMENTS
1	ARE VENTILATORS TOGETHER WITH CLOSING APPLIANCES IN GOOD CONDITION?				
2	IS HULL FREE OF DAMAGES?				
3	ARE DRAUGHT MARKS VISIBLE?				
4	ARE AIR PIPES IN GOOD CONDITION?				
5	ARE COAMINGS AND HATCH COVERS CHECKED?				
6					
7					
8					
9					
10					

NOTES

SHIP MAINTENANCE CHECKLIST

NAME OF SHIP:

MAKE: MODEL:

NAME OF OWNER:

PHONE NO: LICENSE NO:

EMAIL:

NAME OF CAPTAIN:

SIGNATURE & DATE:

GENERAL CHECKLIST

		YES	NO	N/A	COMMENTS
1	ARE OPERATING INSTRUCTIONS PROVIDED WITH IMO SYMBOLS?				
2	ARE FIRE DRILLS BEING HELD AS REQUIRED?				
3	ARE OFFICERS FAMILIAR WITH EMERGENCY STEERING GEAR?				
4					
5					
6					
7					
8					
9					
10					

LIFESAVING EQUIPMENT CHECKLIST

		YES	NO	N/A	COMMENTS
1	ARE SIDE BENCHES IN GOOD CONDITION?				
2	IS LIFEBOAT STERN FRAME IN GOOD CONDITION?				
3	ARE LIFEBOATS BILGES CLEAN?				
4	IS LIFEBOAT ENGINE IN GOOD CONDITION?				
5	ARE LIFEBOAT OARS IN GOOD CONDITION?				
6	ARE LIFEBOATS CORRECTLY STOWED IN DAVIT?				
7	HAVE DAVIT LIMIT SWITCHES BEEN TESTED?				
8					
9					
10					

FIRE FIGHTING CHECKLIST

		YES	NO	N/A	COMMENTS
1	IS THE MAIN FIRE LINE IN GOOD CONDITION?				
2	ARE A REQUIRED NUMBER OF PORTABLE FIRE EXTINGUISHERS AVAILABLE?				
3	ARE FIRE DAMPERS AND DOORS IN GOOD CONDITION?				
4	ARE FIRE ALARM AND DETECTION SYSTEMS WORKING WELL?				
5	ARE BREATHING APPARATUS IN GOOD CONDITION?				
6					
7					
8					
9					
10					

LOAD LINE CHECKLIST

		YES	NO	N/A	COMMENTS
1	ARE VENTILATORS TOGETHER WITH CLOSING APPLIANCES IN GOOD CONDITION?				
2	IS HULL FREE OF DAMAGES?				
3	ARE DRAUGHT MARKS VISIBLE?				
4	ARE AIR PIPES IN GOOD CONDITION?				
5	ARE COAMINGS AND HATCH COVERS CHECKED?				
6					
7					
8					
9					
10					

NOTES

SHIP MAINTENANCE CHECKLIST

NAME OF SHIP:	
MAKE:	MODEL:
NAME OF OWNER:	
PHONE NO:	LICENSE NO:
EMAIL:	
NAME OF CAPTAIN:	
SIGNATURE & DATE:	

GENERAL CHECKLIST

		YES	NO	N/A	COMMENTS
1	ARE OPERATING INSTRUCTIONS PROVIDED WITH IMO SYMBOLS?				
2	ARE FIRE DRILLS BEING HELD AS REQUIRED?				
3	ARE OFFICERS FAMILIAR WITH EMERGENCY STEERING GEAR?				
4					
5					
6					
7					
8					
9					
10					

LIFESAVING EQUIPMENT CHECKLIST

		YES	NO	N/A	COMMENTS
1	ARE SIDE BENCHES IN GOOD CONDITION?				
2	IS LIFEBOAT STERN FRAME IN GOOD CONDITION?				
3	ARE LIFEBOATS BILGES CLEAN?				
4	IS LIFEBOAT ENGINE IN GOOD CONDITION?				
5	ARE LIFEBOAT OARS IN GOOD CONDITION?				
6	ARE LIFEBOATS CORRECTLY STOWED IN DAVIT?				
7	HAVE DAVIT LIMIT SWITCHES BEEN TESTED?				
8					
9					
10					

FIRE FIGHTING CHECKLIST

		YES	NO	N/A	COMMENTS
1	IS THE MAIN FIRE LINE IN GOOD CONDITION?				
2	ARE A REQUIRED NUMBER OF PORTABLE FIRE EXTINGUISHERS AVAILABLE?				
3	ARE FIRE DAMPERS AND DOORS IN GOOD CONDITION?				
4	ARE FIRE ALARM AND DETECTION SYSTEMS WORKING WELL?				
5	ARE BREATHING APPARATUS IN GOOD CONDITION?				
6					
7					
8					
9					
10					

LOAD LINE CHECKLIST

		YES	NO	N/A	COMMENTS
1	ARE VENTILATORS TOGETHER WITH CLOSING APPLIANCES IN GOOD CONDITION?				
2	IS HULL FREE OF DAMAGES?				
3	ARE DRAUGHT MARKS VISIBLE?				
4	ARE AIR PIPES IN GOOD CONDITION?				
5	ARE COAMINGS AND HATCH COVERS CHECKED?				
6					
7					
8					
9					
10					

NOTES

SHIP MAINTENANCE CHECKLIST

NAME OF SHIP:

MAKE: | MODEL:

NAME OF OWNER:

PHONE NO: | LICENSE NO:

EMAIL:

NAME OF CAPTAIN:

SIGNATURE & DATE:

GENERAL CHECKLIST

		YES	NO	N/A	COMMENTS
1	ARE OPERATING INSTRUCTIONS PROVIDED WITH IMO SYMBOLS?				
2	ARE FIRE DRILLS BEING HELD AS REQUIRED?				
3	ARE OFFICERS FAMILIAR WITH EMERGENCY STEERING GEAR?				
4					
5					
6					
7					
8					
9					
10					

LIFESAVING EQUIPMENT CHECKLIST

		YES	NO	N/A	COMMENTS
1	ARE SIDE BENCHES IN GOOD CONDITION?				
2	IS LIFEBOAT STERN FRAME IN GOOD CONDITION?				
3	ARE LIFEBOATS BILGES CLEAN?				
4	IS LIFEBOAT ENGINE IN GOOD CONDITION?				
5	ARE LIFEBOAT OARS IN GOOD CONDITION?				
6	ARE LIFEBOATS CORRECTLY STOWED IN DAVIT?				
7	HAVE DAVIT LIMIT SWITCHES BEEN TESTED?				
8					
9					
10					

FIRE FIGHTING CHECKLIST

		YES	NO	N/A	COMMENTS
1	IS THE MAIN FIRE LINE IN GOOD CONDITION?				
2	ARE A REQUIRED NUMBER OF PORTABLE FIRE EXTINGUISHERS AVAILABLE?				
3	ARE FIRE DAMPERS AND DOORS IN GOOD CONDITION?				
4	ARE FIRE ALARM AND DETECTION SYSTEMS WORKING WELL?				
5	ARE BREATHING APPARATUS IN GOOD CONDITION?				
6					
7					
8					
9					
10					

LOAD LINE CHECKLIST

		YES	NO	N/A	COMMENTS
1	ARE VENTILATORS TOGETHER WITH CLOSING APPLIANCES IN GOOD CONDITION?				
2	IS HULL FREE OF DAMAGES?				
3	ARE DRAUGHT MARKS VISIBLE?				
4	ARE AIR PIPES IN GOOD CONDITION?				
5	ARE COAMINGS AND HATCH COVERS CHECKED?				
6					
7					
8					
9					
10					

NOTES

SHIP MAINTENANCE CHECKLIST

NAME OF SHIP:	
MAKE:	MODEL:
NAME OF OWNER:	
PHONE NO:	LICENSE NO:
EMAIL:	
NAME OF CAPTAIN:	
SIGNATURE & DATE:	

GENERAL CHECKLIST

		YES	NO	N/A	COMMENTS
1	ARE OPERATING INSTRUCTIONS PROVIDED WITH IMO SYMBOLS?				
2	ARE FIRE DRILLS BEING HELD AS REQUIRED?				
3	ARE OFFICERS FAMILIAR WITH EMERGENCY STEERING GEAR?				
4					
5					
6					
7					
8					
9					
10					

LIFESAVING EQUIPMENT CHECKLIST

		YES	NO	N/A	COMMENTS
1	ARE SIDE BENCHES IN GOOD CONDITION?				
2	IS LIFEBOAT STERN FRAME IN GOOD CONDITION?				
3	ARE LIFEBOATS BILGES CLEAN?				
4	IS LIFEBOAT ENGINE IN GOOD CONDITION?				
5	ARE LIFEBOAT OARS IN GOOD CONDITION?				
6	ARE LIFEBOATS CORRECTLY STOWED IN DAVIT?				
7	HAVE DAVIT LIMIT SWITCHES BEEN TESTED?				
8					
9					
10					

FIRE FIGHTING CHECKLIST

		YES	NO	N/A	COMMENTS
1	IS THE MAIN FIRE LINE IN GOOD CONDITION?				
2	ARE A REQUIRED NUMBER OF PORTABLE FIRE EXTINGUISHERS AVAILABLE?				
3	ARE FIRE DAMPERS AND DOORS IN GOOD CONDITION?				
4	ARE FIRE ALARM AND DETECTION SYSTEMS WORKING WELL?				
5	ARE BREATHING APPARATUS IN GOOD CONDITION?				
6					
7					
8					
9					
10					

LOAD LINE CHECKLIST

		YES	NO	N/A	COMMENTS
1	ARE VENTILATORS TOGETHER WITH CLOSING APPLIANCES IN GOOD CONDITION?				
2	IS HULL FREE OF DAMAGES?				
3	ARE DRAUGHT MARKS VISIBLE?				
4	ARE AIR PIPES IN GOOD CONDITION?				
5	ARE COAMINGS AND HATCH COVERS CHECKED?				
6					
7					
8					
9					
10					

NOTES

SHIP MAINTENANCE CHECKLIST

NAME OF SHIP:

MAKE: | MODEL:

NAME OF OWNER:

PHONE NO: | LICENSE NO:

EMAIL:

NAME OF CAPTAIN:

SIGNATURE & DATE:

GENERAL CHECKLIST

		YES	NO	N/A	COMMENTS
1	ARE OPERATING INSTRUCTIONS PROVIDED WITH IMO SYMBOLS?				
2	ARE FIRE DRILLS BEING HELD AS REQUIRED?				
3	ARE OFFICERS FAMILIAR WITH EMERGENCY STEERING GEAR?				
4					
5					
6					
7					
8					
9					
10					

LIFESAVING EQUIPMENT CHECKLIST

		YES	NO	N/A	COMMENTS
1	ARE SIDE BENCHES IN GOOD CONDITION?				
2	IS LIFEBOAT STERN FRAME IN GOOD CONDITION?				
3	ARE LIFEBOATS BILGES CLEAN?				
4	IS LIFEBOAT ENGINE IN GOOD CONDITION?				
5	ARE LIFEBOAT OARS IN GOOD CONDITION?				
6	ARE LIFEBOATS CORRECTLY STOWED IN DAVIT?				
7	HAVE DAVIT LIMIT SWITCHES BEEN TESTED?				
8					
9					
10					

FIRE FIGHTING CHECKLIST

		YES	NO	N/A	COMMENTS
1	IS THE MAIN FIRE LINE IN GOOD CONDITION?				
2	ARE A REQUIRED NUMBER OF PORTABLE FIRE EXTINGUISHERS AVAILABLE?				
3	ARE FIRE DAMPERS AND DOORS IN GOOD CONDITION?				
4	ARE FIRE ALARM AND DETECTION SYSTEMS WORKING WELL?				
5	ARE BREATHING APPARATUS IN GOOD CONDITION?				
6					
7					
8					
9					
10					

LOAD LINE CHECKLIST

		YES	NO	N/A	COMMENTS
1	ARE VENTILATORS TOGETHER WITH CLOSING APPLIANCES IN GOOD CONDITION?				
2	IS HULL FREE OF DAMAGES?				
3	ARE DRAUGHT MARKS VISIBLE?				
4	ARE AIR PIPES IN GOOD CONDITION?				
5	ARE COAMINGS AND HATCH COVERS CHECKED?				
6					
7					
8					
9					
10					

NOTES

SHIP MAINTENANCE CHECKLIST

NAME OF SHIP:

MAKE: | MODEL:

NAME OF OWNER:

PHONE NO: | LICENSE NO:

EMAIL:

NAME OF CAPTAIN:

SIGNATURE & DATE:

GENERAL CHECKLIST

		YES	NO	N/A	COMMENTS
1	ARE OPERATING INSTRUCTIONS PROVIDED WITH IMO SYMBOLS?				
2	ARE FIRE DRILLS BEING HELD AS REQUIRED?				
3	ARE OFFICERS FAMILIAR WITH EMERGENCY STEERING GEAR?				
4					
5					
6					
7					
8					
9					
10					

LIFESAVING EQUIPMENT CHECKLIST

		YES	NO	N/A	COMMENTS
1	ARE SIDE BENCHES IN GOOD CONDITION?				
2	IS LIFEBOAT STERN FRAME IN GOOD CONDITION?				
3	ARE LIFEBOATS BILGES CLEAN?				
4	IS LIFEBOAT ENGINE IN GOOD CONDITION?				
5	ARE LIFEBOAT OARS IN GOOD CONDITION?				
6	ARE LIFEBOATS CORRECTLY STOWED IN DAVIT?				
7	HAVE DAVIT LIMIT SWITCHES BEEN TESTED?				
8					
9					
10					

FIRE FIGHTING CHECKLIST

		YES	NO	N/A	COMMENTS
1	IS THE MAIN FIRE LINE IN GOOD CONDITION?				
2	ARE A REQUIRED NUMBER OF PORTABLE FIRE EXTINGUISHERS AVAILABLE?				
3	ARE FIRE DAMPERS AND DOORS IN GOOD CONDITION?				
4	ARE FIRE ALARM AND DETECTION SYSTEMS WORKING WELL?				
5	ARE BREATHING APPARATUS IN GOOD CONDITION?				
6					
7					
8					
9					
10					

LOAD LINE CHECKLIST

		YES	NO	N/A	COMMENTS
1	ARE VENTILATORS TOGETHER WITH CLOSING APPLIANCES IN GOOD CONDITION?				
2	IS HULL FREE OF DAMAGES?				
3	ARE DRAUGHT MARKS VISIBLE?				
4	ARE AIR PIPES IN GOOD CONDITION?				
5	ARE COAMINGS AND HATCH COVERS CHECKED?				
6					
7					
8					
9					
10					

NOTES

SHIP MAINTENANCE CHECKLIST

NAME OF SHIP:	
MAKE:	MODEL:
NAME OF OWNER:	
PHONE NO:	LICENSE NO:
EMAIL:	
NAME OF CAPTAIN:	
SIGNATURE & DATE:	

GENERAL CHECKLIST

		YES	NO	N/A	COMMENTS
1	ARE OPERATING INSTRUCTIONS PROVIDED WITH IMO SYMBOLS?				
2	ARE FIRE DRILLS BEING HELD AS REQUIRED?				
3	ARE OFFICERS FAMILIAR WITH EMERGENCY STEERING GEAR?				
4					
5					
6					
7					
8					
9					
10					

LIFESAVING EQUIPMENT CHECKLIST

		YES	NO	N/A	COMMENTS
1	ARE SIDE BENCHES IN GOOD CONDITION?				
2	IS LIFEBOAT STERN FRAME IN GOOD CONDITION?				
3	ARE LIFEBOATS BILGES CLEAN?				
4	IS LIFEBOAT ENGINE IN GOOD CONDITION?				
5	ARE LIFEBOAT OARS IN GOOD CONDITION?				
6	ARE LIFEBOATS CORRECTLY STOWED IN DAVIT?				
7	HAVE DAVIT LIMIT SWITCHES BEEN TESTED?				
8					
9					
10					

FIRE FIGHTING CHECKLIST

		YES	NO	N/A	COMMENTS
1	IS THE MAIN FIRE LINE IN GOOD CONDITION?				
2	ARE A REQUIRED NUMBER OF PORTABLE FIRE EXTINGUISHERS AVAILABLE?				
3	ARE FIRE DAMPERS AND DOORS IN GOOD CONDITION?				
4	ARE FIRE ALARM AND DETECTION SYSTEMS WORKING WELL?				
5	ARE BREATHING APPARATUS IN GOOD CONDITION?				
6					
7					
8					
9					
10					

LOAD LINE CHECKLIST

		YES	NO	N/A	COMMENTS
1	ARE VENTILATORS TOGETHER WITH CLOSING APPLIANCES IN GOOD CONDITION?				
2	IS HULL FREE OF DAMAGES?				
3	ARE DRAUGHT MARKS VISIBLE?				
4	ARE AIR PIPES IN GOOD CONDITION?				
5	ARE COAMINGS AND HATCH COVERS CHECKED?				
6					
7					
8					
9					
10					

NOTES

SHIP MAINTENANCE CHECKLIST

NAME OF SHIP:	
MAKE:	MODEL:
NAME OF OWNER:	
PHONE NO:	LICENSE NO:
EMAIL:	
NAME OF CAPTAIN:	
SIGNATURE & DATE:	

GENERAL CHECKLIST

		YES	NO	N/A	COMMENTS
1	ARE OPERATING INSTRUCTIONS PROVIDED WITH IMO SYMBOLS?				
2	ARE FIRE DRILLS BEING HELD AS REQUIRED?				
3	ARE OFFICERS FAMILIAR WITH EMERGENCY STEERING GEAR?				
4					
5					
6					
7					
8					
9					
10					

LIFESAVING EQUIPMENT CHECKLIST

		YES	NO	N/A	COMMENTS
1	ARE SIDE BENCHES IN GOOD CONDITION?				
2	IS LIFEBOAT STERN FRAME IN GOOD CONDITION?				
3	ARE LIFEBOATS BILGES CLEAN?				
4	IS LIFEBOAT ENGINE IN GOOD CONDITION?				
5	ARE LIFEBOAT OARS IN GOOD CONDITION?				
6	ARE LIFEBOATS CORRECTLY STOWED IN DAVIT?				
7	HAVE DAVIT LIMIT SWITCHES BEEN TESTED?				
8					
9					
10					

FIRE FIGHTING CHECKLIST

		YES	NO	N/A	COMMENTS
1	IS THE MAIN FIRE LINE IN GOOD CONDITION?				
2	ARE A REQUIRED NUMBER OF PORTABLE FIRE EXTINGUISHERS AVAILABLE?				
3	ARE FIRE DAMPERS AND DOORS IN GOOD CONDITION?				
4	ARE FIRE ALARM AND DETECTION SYSTEMS WORKING WELL?				
5	ARE BREATHING APPARATUS IN GOOD CONDITION?				
6					
7					
8					
9					
10					

LOAD LINE CHECKLIST

		YES	NO	N/A	COMMENTS
1	ARE VENTILATORS TOGETHER WITH CLOSING APPLIANCES IN GOOD CONDITION?				
2	IS HULL FREE OF DAMAGES?				
3	ARE DRAUGHT MARKS VISIBLE?				
4	ARE AIR PIPES IN GOOD CONDITION?				
5	ARE COAMINGS AND HATCH COVERS CHECKED?				
6					
7					
8					
9					
10					

NOTES

SHIP MAINTENANCE CHECKLIST

NAME OF SHIP:	
MAKE:	MODEL:
NAME OF OWNER:	
PHONE NO:	LICENSE NO:
EMAIL:	
NAME OF CAPTAIN:	
SIGNATURE & DATE:	

GENERAL CHECKLIST

		YES	NO	N/A	COMMENTS
1	ARE OPERATING INSTRUCTIONS PROVIDED WITH IMO SYMBOLS?				
2	ARE FIRE DRILLS BEING HELD AS REQUIRED?				
3	ARE OFFICERS FAMILIAR WITH EMERGENCY STEERING GEAR?				
4					
5					
6					
7					
8					
9					
10					

LIFESAVING EQUIPMENT CHECKLIST

		YES	NO	N/A	COMMENTS
1	ARE SIDE BENCHES IN GOOD CONDITION?				
2	IS LIFEBOAT STERN FRAME IN GOOD CONDITION?				
3	ARE LIFEBOATS BILGES CLEAN?				
4	IS LIFEBOAT ENGINE IN GOOD CONDITION?				
5	ARE LIFEBOAT OARS IN GOOD CONDITION?				
6	ARE LIFEBOATS CORRECTLY STOWED IN DAVIT?				
7	HAVE DAVIT LIMIT SWITCHES BEEN TESTED?				
8					
9					
10					

FIRE FIGHTING CHECKLIST

		YES	NO	N/A	COMMENTS
1	IS THE MAIN FIRE LINE IN GOOD CONDITION?				
2	ARE A REQUIRED NUMBER OF PORTABLE FIRE EXTINGUISHERS AVAILABLE?				
3	ARE FIRE DAMPERS AND DOORS IN GOOD CONDITION?				
4	ARE FIRE ALARM AND DETECTION SYSTEMS WORKING WELL?				
5	ARE BREATHING APPARATUS IN GOOD CONDITION?				
6					
7					
8					
9					
10					

LOAD LINE CHECKLIST

		YES	NO	N/A	COMMENTS
1	ARE VENTILATORS TOGETHER WITH CLOSING APPLIANCES IN GOOD CONDITION?				
2	IS HULL FREE OF DAMAGES?				
3	ARE DRAUGHT MARKS VISIBLE?				
4	ARE AIR PIPES IN GOOD CONDITION?				
5	ARE COAMINGS AND HATCH COVERS CHECKED?				
6					
7					
8					
9					
10					

NOTES

SHIP MAINTENANCE CHECKLIST

NAME OF SHIP:	
MAKE:	MODEL:
NAME OF OWNER:	
PHONE NO:	LICENSE NO:
EMAIL:	
NAME OF CAPTAIN:	
SIGNATURE & DATE:	

GENERAL CHECKLIST

		YES	NO	N/A	COMMENTS
1	ARE OPERATING INSTRUCTIONS PROVIDED WITH IMO SYMBOLS?				
2	ARE FIRE DRILLS BEING HELD AS REQUIRED?				
3	ARE OFFICERS FAMILIAR WITH EMERGENCY STEERING GEAR?				
4					
5					
6					
7					
8					
9					
10					

LIFESAVING EQUIPMENT CHECKLIST

		YES	NO	N/A	COMMENTS
1	ARE SIDE BENCHES IN GOOD CONDITION?				
2	IS LIFEBOAT STERN FRAME IN GOOD CONDITION?				
3	ARE LIFEBOATS BILGES CLEAN?				
4	IS LIFEBOAT ENGINE IN GOOD CONDITION?				
5	ARE LIFEBOAT OARS IN GOOD CONDITION?				
6	ARE LIFEBOATS CORRECTLY STOWED IN DAVIT?				
7	HAVE DAVIT LIMIT SWITCHES BEEN TESTED?				
8					
9					
10					

FIRE FIGHTING CHECKLIST

		YES	NO	N/A	COMMENTS
1	IS THE MAIN FIRE LINE IN GOOD CONDITION?				
2	ARE A REQUIRED NUMBER OF PORTABLE FIRE EXTINGUISHERS AVAILABLE?				
3	ARE FIRE DAMPERS AND DOORS IN GOOD CONDITION?				
4	ARE FIRE ALARM AND DETECTION SYSTEMS WORKING WELL?				
5	ARE BREATHING APPARATUS IN GOOD CONDITION?				
6					
7					
8					
9					
10					

LOAD LINE CHECKLIST

		YES	NO	N/A	COMMENTS
1	ARE VENTILATORS TOGETHER WITH CLOSING APPLIANCES IN GOOD CONDITION?				
2	IS HULL FREE OF DAMAGES?				
3	ARE DRAUGHT MARKS VISIBLE?				
4	ARE AIR PIPES IN GOOD CONDITION?				
5	ARE COAMINGS AND HATCH COVERS CHECKED?				
6					
7					
8					
9					
10					

NOTES

SHIP MAINTENANCE CHECKLIST

NAME OF SHIP:	
MAKE:	MODEL:
NAME OF OWNER:	
PHONE NO:	LICENSE NO:
EMAIL:	
NAME OF CAPTAIN:	
SIGNATURE & DATE:	

GENERAL CHECKLIST

		YES	NO	N/A	COMMENTS
1	ARE OPERATING INSTRUCTIONS PROVIDED WITH IMO SYMBOLS?				
2	ARE FIRE DRILLS BEING HELD AS REQUIRED?				
3	ARE OFFICERS FAMILIAR WITH EMERGENCY STEERING GEAR?				
4					
5					
6					
7					
8					
9					
10					

LIFESAVING EQUIPMENT CHECKLIST

		YES	NO	N/A	COMMENTS
1	ARE SIDE BENCHES IN GOOD CONDITION?				
2	IS LIFEBOAT STERN FRAME IN GOOD CONDITION?				
3	ARE LIFEBOATS BILGES CLEAN?				
4	IS LIFEBOAT ENGINE IN GOOD CONDITION?				
5	ARE LIFEBOAT OARS IN GOOD CONDITION?				
6	ARE LIFEBOATS CORRECTLY STOWED IN DAVIT?				
7	HAVE DAVIT LIMIT SWITCHES BEEN TESTED?				
8					
9					
10					

FIRE FIGHTING CHECKLIST

		YES	NO	N/A	COMMENTS
1	IS THE MAIN FIRE LINE IN GOOD CONDITION?				
2	ARE A REQUIRED NUMBER OF PORTABLE FIRE EXTINGUISHERS AVAILABLE?				
3	ARE FIRE DAMPERS AND DOORS IN GOOD CONDITION?				
4	ARE FIRE ALARM AND DETECTION SYSTEMS WORKING WELL?				
5	ARE BREATHING APPARATUS IN GOOD CONDITION?				
6					
7					
8					
9					
10					

LOAD LINE CHECKLIST

		YES	NO	N/A	COMMENTS
1	ARE VENTILATORS TOGETHER WITH CLOSING APPLIANCES IN GOOD CONDITION?				
2	IS HULL FREE OF DAMAGES?				
3	ARE DRAUGHT MARKS VISIBLE?				
4	ARE AIR PIPES IN GOOD CONDITION?				
5	ARE COAMINGS AND HATCH COVERS CHECKED?				
6					
7					
8					
9					
10					

NOTES

SHIP MAINTENANCE CHECKLIST

NAME OF SHIP:

MAKE:	MODEL:

NAME OF OWNER:

PHONE NO:	LICENSE NO:

EMAIL:

NAME OF CAPTAIN:

SIGNATURE & DATE:

GENERAL CHECKLIST

		YES	NO	N/A	COMMENTS
1	ARE OPERATING INSTRUCTIONS PROVIDED WITH IMO SYMBOLS?				
2	ARE FIRE DRILLS BEING HELD AS REQUIRED?				
3	ARE OFFICERS FAMILIAR WITH EMERGENCY STEERING GEAR?				
4					
5					
6					
7					
8					
9					
10					

LIFESAVING EQUIPMENT CHECKLIST

		YES	NO	N/A	COMMENTS
1	ARE SIDE BENCHES IN GOOD CONDITION?				
2	IS LIFEBOAT STERN FRAME IN GOOD CONDITION?				
3	ARE LIFEBOATS BILGES CLEAN?				
4	IS LIFEBOAT ENGINE IN GOOD CONDITION?				
5	ARE LIFEBOAT OARS IN GOOD CONDITION?				
6	ARE LIFEBOATS CORRECTLY STOWED IN DAVIT?				
7	HAVE DAVIT LIMIT SWITCHES BEEN TESTED?				
8					
9					
10					

FIRE FIGHTING CHECKLIST

		YES	NO	N/A	COMMENTS
1	IS THE MAIN FIRE LINE IN GOOD CONDITION?				
2	ARE A REQUIRED NUMBER OF PORTABLE FIRE EXTINGUISHERS AVAILABLE?				
3	ARE FIRE DAMPERS AND DOORS IN GOOD CONDITION?				
4	ARE FIRE ALARM AND DETECTION SYSTEMS WORKING WELL?				
5	ARE BREATHING APPARATUS IN GOOD CONDITION?				
6					
7					
8					
9					
10					

LOAD LINE CHECKLIST

		YES	NO	N/A	COMMENTS
1	ARE VENTILATORS TOGETHER WITH CLOSING APPLIANCES IN GOOD CONDITION?				
2	IS HULL FREE OF DAMAGES?				
3	ARE DRAUGHT MARKS VISIBLE?				
4	ARE AIR PIPES IN GOOD CONDITION?				
5	ARE COAMINGS AND HATCH COVERS CHECKED?				
6					
7					
8					
9					
10					

NOTES

NOTES

Made in the USA
Monee, IL
08 September 2022

13539976R00070